'This important book demonstrates that advances in gender equality are possible within organizations and communities. It also demonstrates that change takes time, the willingness of organizations and communities to learn and adapt, and a dedicated team to promote change. The approach of the Gender Quality Action Learning team was both practical (learning from problems) and strategic (aiming for structural change): reflecting and embodying Maxine Molyneux's framework of "practical" and "strategic" interests of women. The results of the Gender Quality Action Learning project are impressive, as well documented in this book. The challenge for BRAC is to sustain the gains made in gender equality while also tackling other inequalities: as the lives and work of women in poor households in Bangladesh are shaped not only by patriarchal gender norms but also by class interests, corporate practices and economic policies.'

Marty Chen, International Coordinator of the WIEGO Network and Lecturer in Public Policy at the Harvard Kennedy School, USA who helped start BRAC's Women's Program in the 1970s

'This book is about one of BRAC's transformational projects in advancing a gender equality and women's empowerment agenda in Bangladesh. It shows that significant headway is possible to change poor women's *condition* and *position* and in mainstreaming gender equality in a large organization within a patriarchal society.'

Ahmed Mushtaque Raza Chowdhury, Vice Chairperson on the BRAC Board of Governors, Bangladesh

'*Advancing Gender Equality in Bangladesh: Twenty Years of BRAC's Gender Quality Action Learning Program* by Rieky Stuart, Aruna Rao, David Kelleher, Sheepa Hafiza, Hasne Ara Begum and Carol Miller (Routledge 2017, forthcoming) provides an in-depth analysis of the history and impact of an extraordinary twenty-year experiment in mainstreaming gender in one of the world's largest NGOs, while also offering readers a practical, tested methodology for building cultures of gender-sensitive change applicable to other organizations. The approach facilitates locally-led problem solving and adaptation to addressing discriminatory gender norms. It starts with problems or issues rather than ready-made solutions, lending itself well to contemporary calls for approaches to development that prioritize learning and adaptation. The authors provide evidence of the link between investments in internal organizational change efforts and changes in program quality and program outcomes for women and communities which have sometimes been illusive in work on gender mainstreaming. The book will be extremely valuable for those researching gender and institutions as well as those working inside organizations to make change happen.'

Professor Naila Kabeer, London School of Economics, UK

Advancing Gender Equality in Bangladesh

In 1994, BRAC, the world's largest NGO, made headlines by putting women's rights centre stage in Bangladesh, one of the poorest countries in the world. The Gender Quality Action Learning (GQAL) Programme was one of the very first large-scale efforts to mainstream gender equality and aimed to weave objectives of gender equality throughout its own microfinance, education and health services.

Advancing Gender Equality in Bangladesh describes the history, implementation and outcome of this major 20-year initiative and discusses the lessons learned throughout the fight to achieve gender equality outcomes in an effort to provide a tangible framework for future organizations interested in promoting gender equality and social inclusion. At a time when many gender equality programs are still relatively young, this book offers a unique opportunity to track 20 years of intervention within a theoretical and cultural context and provides a platform for ongoing discussion about the roles of empowerment and gender transformation as agents for social change.

This book provides an in-depth analysis of how strategies for change have operated in practice and will be of considerable interest to students, researchers and practitioners of international development, gender studies and social justice theory as well as those interested in a new practical methodology of the Gender at Work Analytical Framework.

Rieky Stuart is an associate of Gender at Work and a consultant in international development and was a member of the original GQAL team.

Aruna Rao is the Co-founder and Executive Director of Gender at Work, an international feminist network committed to ending discrimination against women and advancing cultures of equality. Aruna was the team leader of the GQAL programme.

David Kelleher is an Associate of Gender at Work and was a member of the original GQAL team at BRAC.

Sheepa Hafiza was the one of the founders of GQAL and was the lead for the programme.

Carol Miller is Knowledge Strategist at Gender at Work, a global network focused on institutional change for gender equality.

Hasne Ara Begum works as Programme Manager for the Gender Justice and Diversity Programme of BRAC in Bangladesh and has 19 years' experience working with government, non-government and international organizations in research, monitoring and evaluation.

Routledge ISS Gender, Sexuality and Development Studies

The *Routledge ISS Gender, Sexuality and Development Studies* series explores the diverse ways in which topics of gender and sexuality relate to international development, both in theory and in practice. The book series aims to publish 'classical' gender, sexuality and development themes – such as the sexual and reproductive rights policy debates on population and sustainable development, adolescence and sex education, and policy on abortion – together with cutting edge work on embodiment, queer theory and innovative strategies of resistance to hegemonic discourses of sexuality and gender. The book series will pay special attention to the role of intergenerational power relations and how they interact with different gendered understandings of sexuality at diverse stages in the life cycle.

Wendy Harcourt leads the international editorial board with her colleagues from the renowned International Institute of Social Studies of Erasmus University, The Netherlands. The Board welcomes book proposals from researchers working in all geographic areas with special interest in research undertaken from feminist grounded theory and with marginalized groups in the global South and North.

To find out more about how to submit a book proposal, please contact the Development Studies Editor, Helena Hurd (Helena.Hurd@tandf.co.uk) or Wendy Harcourt (harcourt@iss.nl).

Global Trends in Land Tenure Reform
Gender Impacts
Edited by Caroline S. Archambault and Annelies Zoomers

Gender, Power and Knowledge for Development
Lata Narayanaswamy

Gender Responsive Budgeting in Fragile States
The Case of Timor-Leste
Monica Costa

Advancing Gender Equality in Bangladesh

Twenty Years of BRAC's Gender Quality
Action Learning Programme

**Rieky Stuart, Aruna Rao, David
Kelleher, Sheepa Hafiza, Carol Miller
and Hasne Ara Begum**

Routledge
Taylor & Francis Group

LONDON AND NEW YORK

First published 2017
by Routledge
2 Park Square, Milton Park, Abingdon, Oxon OX14 4RN

and by Routledge
711 Third Avenue, New York, NY 10017

Routledge is an imprint of the Taylor & Francis Group, an informa business

British Library Cataloguing in Publication Data
A catalogue record for this book is available from the British Library

Library of Congress Cataloging in Publication Data
A catalog record for this book has been requested

ISBN: 978-1-138-72026-8 (hbk)
ISBN: 978-1-315-19508-7 (ebk)

Typeset in Bembo
by Taylor & Francis Books

Printed and bound by CPI Group (UK) Ltd, Croydon, CR0 4YY

Contents

Illustrations

Figures

Tables

Contributors

Rieky Stuart was a member of the original GQAL team. She is an associate of Gender at Work and a consultant in international development. She was Executive Director of Oxfam Canada from 1999 to 2005, has previously served as Deputy Director for the Canadian Council for International Cooperation, and also taught at St Francis Xavier University's Coady International Institute.

Aruna Rao was the team leader of the original GQAL programme. She is the Co-founder and Executive Director of Gender at Work, an international feminist network committed to ending discrimination against women and advancing cultures of equality. She is an expert in gender and development with over 30 years' experience in pioneering new approaches to gender and institutional change, working alongside government, United Nations and international development agencies. She holds a Ph.D. in Educational Administration from Columbia University, New York.

David Kelleher was a member of the original GQAL Team at BRAC. He is a co-founder and Senior Associate of Gender at Work, a global knowledge and capacity-building network on institutional change for gender equality. He has worked with numerous organizations in Canada and internationally over the past 40 years, helping them build their capacity for social change.

Sheepa Hafiza was the one of the founders of GQAL and was the lead for the programme. She was responsible for a variety of innovative approaches to gender and change programmes from 1992 to 2016 in BRAC. She has received several awards, including the Communication for Sustainable Social Change Award at the University of Massachusetts, to honour her work on migrant rights, and the Best Practice Award for Gender Norm Change. Her international publications are on gender justice, policy advocacy for extreme poverty reduction, climate resilience and empowering livelihoods for women.

Carol Miller is Knowledge Strategist at Gender at Work, a global network focused on institutional change for gender equality. She has previously worked for UNRISD, ActionAid and Oxfam. She holds a D.Phil. from

Oxford University and a graduate degree in Policy and Program Evaluation from Carleton University, Canada.

Hasne Ara Begum works as Programme Manager for the Gender Justice and Diversity Programme of BRAC in Bangladesh and has 19 years' experience working with government, non-government and international organizations in research, monitoring and evaluation. She is also active in regional and national women's rights movements, policy advocacy networks and platforms.

Foreword

BRAC's primary concern is the dynamics of poverty. Poor people are poor because they are powerless. We need to build societies where everyone has a chance. We need equality of opportunity, not necessarily of wealth, so everyone has an opportunity to rise through his or her hard work. That means providing quality education to children and eradicating extreme poverty. This is the next generation of challenges we must face and win. For the first time in history, though, I think that we can.

In my life, however, gender equality is the unfinished agenda and I think it will remain so for a long time to come. It is very hard work, but vital. BRAC has provided women and men with tools to enable them to defeat poverty – tools such as microfinance, healthcare, family planning services and education. We began with pilot projects in small areas, but as soon as we knew they were effective, we replicated them nationally. Changing hearts and minds is not easy, however. As facilitators of change, BRAC staff themselves needed to understand the meaning of gender equality and to practise those values in their day-to-day work and relationships. Through the Gender Quality Action Learning (GQAL) programme, BRAC experimented with building a culture of equality within BRAC and in the communities in which we work. From the start, I believed that GQAL had the power to change BRAC as it took on the challenge of greater gender equality within BRAC and improving the quality of our programmes with rigour and care.

This book tells the GQAL story from the vantage point of time – 20 years, in fact. GQAL, which started in 1994, continues today. It can be thought of as a longstanding effort in gender mainstreaming. This book describes the foundational work in setting up the programme, and analyses how the programme generated learning and change in its participants, in BRAC's ways of working, and in the lives of the women and men BRAC serves. It concludes with a reflection on the implications of GQAL's contributions to the challenges BRAC faces today.

The struggles and tensions of building a culture of equality have not been resolved. I do not believe that small is beautiful. I always wanted to have a national impact on poverty. Maintaining a dual focus on rapid expansion and making qualitative changes in power dynamics and patriarchy, is a tough balancing act. BRAC's experience in holding these tensions in the context of growth as well as its successes and its challenges, is instructive to us as we forge a pathway for the future. I believe it would also be of interest to academics and development practitioners in Bangladesh and elsewhere in the world who are grappling with poverty eradication and cultural change.

I should like to express my sincere thanks to Sheepa Hafiza and BRAC's Gender Justice and Diversity Team for their continuous efforts to challenge and change BRAC's organisational culture and steer its programmatic work towards greater equity and inclusion. I also thank Dr Aruna Rao, Rieky Stuart and David Kelleher, along with BRAC's GQAL Team, for their valuable contributions.

Sir Fazle Hasan Abed
Founder and Chairperson
BRAC

brac

Acknowledgements

The authors would like to thank Sir Fazle Hasan Abed, KCMG, the Founder and Chairperson of BRAC, whose inspiration, support, leadership and guidance were the basis of the work described in this book.

The authors would also like to thank BRAC for supporting the production of this book; Gender at Work for its commitment to learning and sharing pathways to promote gender equality; and the staff of the Gender Justice and Diversity Division of BRAC for their thoughtful reflection and insights into GQAL and BRAC, as well as their diligent stewardship of the research and information compiled in this book. Thanks are also due to Dr Ahmed Mushtaque Raza Chowdhury, Vice-Chairperson of BRAC; Dr Muhammed Musa, Executive Director of BRAC; S.N. Koiry, CFO, BRAC and BRAC International; and Asif Saleh, the Senior Director for Strategy, Communication and Empowerment, who supported and encouraged the production of this book. We are also grateful for the valuable feedback and comments we received from early readers Diana Rivington and Bessa Whitmore; and for the support of the team at Routledge, particularly Kelly Watkins. Finally, our thanks to our wonderful editor, Priya Kvam.

Abbreviations

AAF	Ayesha Abed Foundation
AC	Area Coordinator
ADP	Adolescent Development Programme
AM	Area Manager
BDP	BRAC Development Programme
BEP	BRAC Education Programme
BTD	BRAC Training Division
CEP	Community Empowerment Programme
CFPR–TUP	Challenging the Frontiers of Poverty Reduction–Targeting the Ultra Poor
CLF	Community Leaders Forum
DSG	Development Support Group
EVAWC	Ending Violence Against Women Committee
FGD	Focus group discussion
GAAC	Gender Awareness and Analysis Course
GADN	Gender and Development Network
GDBC	Gram Daridra Bimochon Committee
GEDT	Gender Equality and Diversity Team
GEWE	Gender Equality and Women's Empowerment
GJD	Gender Justice and Diversity Unit
GJE	Gender Justice Educator
GQAL	Gender Quality Action Learning
HDI	Human Development Index
HRLE	Human Rights and Legal Education
KAP	Knowledge, attitude and practice
M&E	Monitoring and evaluation
MDG	Millennium Development Goal
MEJNIN	Meyeder Jonno Nirapod Nagorikotto (Safe Citizenship for Girls)
MP	Member of Parliament
NFEP	Non-Formal Education Programme
NGO	Non-governmental organization
NI	New Institutional

OECD	Organization for Economic Cooperation and Development
OTEP	Oral (Rehydration) Therapy Extension Programme
PO	Programme Officer
POSITION	Enhancing a Positive Life Programme
PS	Palli Shamaj
RCT	Randomized control trial
RDP	Rural Development Programme
RED	Research and Evaluation Division
RM	Regional Manager
RSP	Road Safety Programme
SAMPRITI	Strengthening Awareness, Mobility, Participation, Rights and Inclusiveness and Transforming Ideology
SHP	Sexual Harassment Policy
SHRC	Sexual Harassment Redressal Committee
SMI	Safe Motherhood Initiative
SS	Shasthaya Shebikas
STUP	Specially Targeted Ultra Poor
TOT	Training of Trainers
UN	United Nations
UP	Union Parishad
VAW	Violence against women
VDC	Village Development Committee
VO	Village Organization
VYE	Volunteer Youth Educator
WAC	Women's Advisory Committee
WGEE	Women and Girls' Economic Empowerment
WHDP	Women's Health and Development Programme
WID	Women in Development

Introduction

In 1994, BRAC launched the Gender Quality Action Learning (GQAL) Programme, an ambitious effort to advance women's empowerment and gender equality. The programme focused on strengthening BRAC staff's capacity for informed and gender-equitable problem-solving and on building an organizational culture that supported BRAC's vision and mission. Later, it focused on addressing gender relations between women and men in the communities in which BRAC provided credit, health and education services, and support for income-generating activities. GQAL was an early, large-scale effort to 'mainstream' gender equality – an approach that was widely endorsed at the Beijing World Conference on Women in 1995, and that remains a core strategy for United Nations (UN), bilateral and non-governmental (NGO) development organizations.

The GQAL Programme unfolded in three main phases (see Appendix 1). From 1994 to 2003, GQAL worked with staff, eventually reaching 16,000 members of staff in 800 Area Offices across the country. From 2001 to 2011, the programme was adapted to work with BRAC members in rural communities in tandem with BRAC's pilot programme to reach ultra-poor clients. From 2012, GQAL has been offered as a stand-alone programme, ultimately covering 300,000 households and touching the lives of over 2 million people.

The GQAL Programme was one of the first efforts to combine feminist analysis, organizational change theory and best thinking about adult learning. It was relatively well resourced, so it was possible to 'dream big' and apply our best thinking to practice. The programme had strong sponsorship within BRAC, but still had to negotiate the realities of organizational life, including a range of beliefs, practices and accountabilities that represented challenges to its effective implementation.

The design, implementation and results of GQAL offer valuable and interesting lessons for development organizations seeking to promote gender equality as an end in itself and as part of their poverty-reduction agendas. It should also be of interest to academics studying the strategies and outcomes of development organizations' efforts to promote gender equality and poverty reduction, including the rise and fall of trends in theory and practice on gender and development over the past 25 years. We believe the story of GQAL will be of particular interest in light of current enthusiasm over what is labelled 'adaptive development' (see O'Neil, 2016). We argue that the approach and methodology of GQAL encapsulates characteristics of adaptive development and, as such, has much to contribute to current debates, if only to remind us that development trends are indeed cyclical.

The four core principles of adaptive development are as follows:

1   to support change led by local stakeholders, not external funders;
2   to start with problems or issues, not with ready-made solutions;
3   to be politically informed and use smart tactics; and
4   to build learning and adaptation into organizations and programmes.

(O'Neil, 2016: 9)

Some have argued that the current adaptive development discourse may be 'gender blind' (Green, 2015, cited in O'Neil, 2016). We argue that GQAL provides a strong example of a tried and tested methodology that facilitates locally led problem-solving, learning and adaptation in the context of work to address root causes of gender inequality.

Development organizations seldom have the opportunity to look back nearly 25 years to track the results of their interventions. This book documents the history and impact of the GQAL Programme – the ideas that animated it; its results and impact on BRAC staff and the organization more widely; and its impacts at the community level. It concludes with reflections on the implications of GQAL for BRAC's approach to gender equality today.

Can you recall an event from 20 years ago and whether it influenced your life – how you thought, what you did, or how you felt? Can you describe that process of change? Did the change affect your workplace life and your personal life, too? These are some of the questions BRAC was interested in exploring with former managers and staff, with GQAL trainers and participants and with village-level participants, all of whom were motivated by the 20-year anniversary of GQAL, and by the imminent retirement of Sheepa Hafiza, who had headed the programme for BRAC since its inception. BRAC wanted to capture this important part of its organizational history, especially for a new generation of managers and staff who lack first-hand knowledge of GQAL's theoretical foundation and its programmatic evolution.

In 2015, we interviewed and surveyed over 600 people who participated in the 1994–2003 GQAL process. The vast majority were able to recall in considerable detail what happened during this process, and what changes it brought about. This in itself is a positive sign of its influence. Our analysis also draws on the numerous reports, evaluations and studies done over the years on BRAC's GQAL Programme, in consultation with staff and in the communities it has served.

The book represents a collective effort of the authors[1] to tell the story of GQAL from the perspective of BRAC staff and of the external gender consultants who supported the processes and have had a sustained relationship with

BRAC over 20 years. The external gender consultants bring knowledge of BRAC and its story, yet are also able to understand this story in relation to their research and experiences of working with more than 100 organizations over the past 25 years to advance the cause of gender equality.

Why should this story be heard? BRAC is the world's largest – and one of the most well-respected – NGOs, currently reaching an estimated 138 million people, with more than 110,000 employees and an annual expenditure of US $1 billion.[2] It has become known globally for its innovative approaches to providing services to the poor, including micro-finance for women. BRAC's approaches to poverty reduction and empowerment have considerable influence across the development sector. From its origins in the 1970s in rural Bangladesh, described in Chapter 1, BRAC has expanded and adapted its model to work in 11 countries. BRAC's journey towards gender equality started with the Sulla Project in 1973, when, recognizing the distinct needs of poor women for empowerment and mutual support, BRAC formed its first women's groups; in 1975, it started the first women's project (with women handicraft producers) in Jamalpur to support women directly in income generation. Since the late 1980s, BRAC has directed its policies and programmes towards achieving gender equality. It has carried out sustained interventions targeting women's – especially rural women's – basic needs and strategic interests through healthcare, legal education, access to credit, gender awareness and training, and more.[3] In 2016, there were nearly 10 million women members of Village Organisations (VOs) – that is, community lending and savings groups – across Bangladesh.[4]

Large service delivery NGOs such as BRAC are unique, but also not exceptional in that *all* development organizations face similar opportunities and challenges in constructing gender-sensitive organizational cultures like those discussed in this book: the obstacles and resistance faced by gender advocates and the strategies employed to overcome these barriers; the trade-offs and strategic choices that must be made and the costs to gender advocates in making them; and the reality that, despite internal commitment and gender accountability mechanisms, organizations can get 'stuck' and may require new and innovative approaches to move things forward. As we argue throughout this book, the complex interrelationship between individual attitudes and behaviours, on the one hand, and organizational policies and practices, on the other, can undermine or enhance efforts to promote gender equality. Creative, context-specific, flexible approaches are required to make these complex relationships more transparent and to create space for effective problem-solving. We offer GQAL as one such tested, successful approach, whilst acknowledging from the outset that the journey has not always been easy.

Working on gender equality in organizations: the state of play in 1994

As the Gender Team began its work in BRAC in 1994, it did so against a background of significant thinking and practice on women's rights and gender equality. Women-in-Development (WID) efforts, which were propelled by the 1975 World Conference on Women in Mexico City and the United Nations Decade for Women (1976–1985), demanded social justice and equity for women. These efforts to establish women as a serious development concern within the debates and frameworks of the day – anti-poverty strategies and the basic needs approaches of the 1980s, followed by the human development approach in the 1990s – and to target resources to women in development efforts led to some gains. But these were limited by women's lack of power, both economic and social, to translate whatever opportunities were available into strategic gains that would change the power relationship between men and women. Leaders of gender and development efforts, in the run-up to the Fourth World Conference on Women in 1995, took stock of the various gender analysis frameworks that were being used to promote gender equality within development institutions (see Razavi and Miller (1995) for a full discussion). Their concern was that the 'relational nature of [women's] subordination had been left largely unexplored' by efforts to integrate women into development (Razavi and Miller, 1995: 12). Their response was to develop alternative frameworks that drew attention to the need to challenge male power and privilege more directly and the ways women and men consciously and unconsciously perpetuated these structures of inequality.

One approach that strongly influenced our thinking in 1994 was the Social Relations Framework (see Kabeer, 1994), with its conceptualization of how social structures, processes and gendered power relations operate to maintain inequalities. The Social Relations Framework mapped how gender discrimination and inequalities are created, maintained and reproduced in institutions (i.e., the household, community, market and state). From this analytical perspective, supporting gender equality for women involved more than reallocating economic resources – the primary mechanism through which development programmes had attempted to integrate women to date – but also required redistributing power (Razavi and Miller, 1995: 28). In other words, proponents of this approach argued, efforts to reallocate economic resources to promote gender equality outcomes (or even to promote economic efficiency) cannot happen without changes in gender relations across the range of institutions through which men and women access these resources.

The Framework begins with the premise that development interventions need to take account of the broad range of relations and institutions through which needs are met – that is, 'the social relations of everyday life' (Pearson, Whitehead, and Young, 1981: x, cited in Razavi and Miller, 1995: 28). From the perspective of social relations analysis, gender is always intertwined with other social relations – gender, class, ethnicity, age, religion, caste and so on cross-cut with one another. Kabeer (1994: 299) was also very clear that '[s]ince power relations between women and men are the product of institutional practice, genuine change entails institutional transformation'.

An analysis put forward by Maxine Molyneux (1985), who distinguished between women's 'condition' and 'position' and women's 'practical' and 'strategic' interests (cited in Kabeer, 1994: 89–91), also influenced our thinking about transformative change. Molyneux (1985: 232) argued that women's 'practical interests are usually a response to immediate perceived need', whereas their strategic gender interests derive 'from the analysis of their subordination and from the formulation of an alternative, more satisfactory set of arrangements from those which exist' (cited in Kabeer, 1994: 90). For example, food and income are practical needs that affect a woman's *condition*, while her status and voice in the community and in her family affect her *position*. If she has a say in how savings are allocated, or if she can get the medical care she needs, she is acting in her strategic interest. Molyneux's conceptualization helps to distinguish between interventions that focus on the conditions of women's daily lives and those that work to transform women's position by challenging structural inequalities and, indeed, helps to explain why so many programmes that focus only on women's condition fail to deliver real change for them.

Development practitioners were beginning to integrate this thinking into gender-training approaches in the 1990s, challenging or adapting popular gender frameworks and tools that had identified the need to pay attention to gender-differentiated roles and access and control over income and other resources. They tended, however, to under-conceptualize the dynamics of gendered power relations in shaping and maintaining gender roles and access to resources (see Miller and Razavi, 1998a; March *et al.*, 1999). In the run-up to the Beijing Conference in 1995, and in the years that followed, gender training was regarded as the panacea for producing gender-equality outcomes in development organizations. Significant resources were devoted to the design and delivery of gender training to increase staff gender awareness and technical skills to carry out gender analysis. This would, it was believed, contribute to improved development practice. It was clear to us at the time, however, that the standard approaches and formats of gender training would not be up to the task, as we understood it.

The GQAL Programme has its epistemological roots in lessons learned from a decade of applying gender-analysis frameworks in various gender-training efforts in a range of development agencies, from state bureaucracies to NGOs. The first international conference on gender training, held in Bergen in 1991, reinforced a growing understanding that women's voices and priorities were systematically marginalized in development institutions, which were themselves gendered in fundamental ways (Rao *et al.*, 1991). The deep structures of these institutions combined a toxic mix of discriminatory norms and values that limited women's participation and voice; thwarted feminist ambitions; and resulted in outcomes that did not work for women. This understanding underscored, for us, the limits of standard gender-training approaches in the absence of attention to deeper, structural issues.

A growing body of research on gender and institutions was exploring, in greater depth, the issues raised at the Bergen conference. This research also influenced our thinking as we reflected on strategies for building BRAC's capacity on gender.[5] Women staff and gender advocates within the NGO sector – even in organizations that had an explicit mandate to empower women – were becoming increasingly frustrated with what they saw as weak 'gender accountability' in their own organizations, which were presumed to have a comparative advantage over other development institutions when it came to reaching the poor and socially marginalized, including women, and in representing their interests.[6]

In her seminal work on gender and development institutions, Anne-Marie Goetz (1992) argued that public administration itself was gendered and that service delivery NGOs had not only failed to provide services equitably, but that organizational structures, outcomes and cultures reflected and promoted the interests of men and served to maintain unequal practices and gendered cultural norms. In her study of five NGOs and three state rural development administrations in Bangladesh, Goetz found that organizational structures reinforced gender divisions by restricting opportunities for women staff or by segregating women into specific categories of work.

Earlier writers had presented similar evidence in pointing out the lack of women in managerial ranks (Kanter, 1977, cited in Acker, 1990) and the marginalization of women's interests in bureaucracies (Staudt, 1990). Joan Acker (1990: 46) attempted to debunk the myth of the sex-neutral bureaucracy, quoting Kanter (1977): 'While organizations were being defined as sex-neutral machines, masculine principles were defining their authority structures.' Acker also developed an analysis that was to be very influential in our thinking. She argued that much of this male domination was locked beneath our awareness in taken-for-granted ideas about jobs, hierarchy and the fact that the 'ideal worker' in any organization is perceived to be a man who can make the organization his first (and at times only) priority. This ideal is stacked against women: a woman with child-rearing responsibilities can never conform to such an image (Acker, 1990).

As 'gender mainstreaming' was beginning to take off in the mid-1990s as a key strategy among development organizations for promoting gender equality, a common set of 'tools' emerged alongside it, including, as we have noted above, conceptual and analytical frameworks for gender analysis and related gender-training programmes, in addition to a push for the development of organizational gender policies, strategies and action plans. Indeed, 'gender mainstreaming' emerged in response to the growing understanding among gender advocates that a diverse and, ideally, integrated set of strategies – one of which was gender training – would be needed to ensure that gender equality was integrated into 'mainstream' development policies and programmes.

As we met as a Gender Team at BRAC in 1994, we worked with this collection of conceptual approaches and strategies. We were asked to do gender training, but were mindful of the discussions at the Bergen conference and aware, in particular, of the ineffectiveness of decanting technical knowledge into staff members without making a connection to the power relations, norms and processes that kept gendered behaviour in place. We wanted learning about gender to be personal and political as well as technical. We believed that learning was not just about acquiring knowledge and changing attitudes, but about behaving differently. We also believed that changing the organization itself was needed for this learning to happen.[7]

The book describes in some detail the approach and methodology we developed for GQAL with staff, documenting how GQAL can be differentiated from conventional gender training. The 'action-learning' feature was an innovation that enabled us to create space to nurture women's and men's agency to identify and combat gender injustice in many forms. This approach is still used successfully by Gender at Work in its action-learning processes with community organizations and NGOs around the world.[8]

GQAL proved extraordinarily effective in shifting attitudes and behaviour in favour of gender equality inside BRAC, as well as in its programmes, where it was adapted and expanded to support work with local communities. Among other changes, we saw that women staff reported greater self-confidence; women and men increasingly recognized women's ability to do BRAC work; there was less harassment of subordinates and peers; and staff were increasingly aware of and responsible for enforcing policies in support of work–life balance. Senior management's sustained support was vital in demonstrating that the organization was serious about gender equality. During the implementation of GQAL inside BRAC, as information was reported about problems identified at the Area Office level, senior managers were often quick to change the policies that were causing problems, or to support the active implementation of policies that had the potential to bring about positive change. This demonstrated to front-line staff that senior managers were serious, and reinforced staff commitment to problem-solving and to working towards changes in attitudes and behaviour. Overall, GQAL contributed to a greater 'culture of learning' in the teams that designed and implemented it, as well as for participants; it strengthened their initiative and capacity to identify and solve problems related to gender inequality.

Efforts to work on gender and organizational change walk a fine line between challenge and co-optation. Alongside what we hope is a compelling story of GQAL-supported change, this book also describes our strategic choices, difficult trade-offs and learning as we pushed for GQAL's implementation and worked to overcome (inevitable) resistance from certain quarters.

Doing 'training' differently in support of organizational change

As described in the early chapters of this book, the Gender Team was invited to work with the Training Division of BRAC to build staff capacity on gender. One of the ideas that influenced the development of GQAL was our understanding that, if we wanted to achieve gender-equality outcomes across BRAC and its programmes, we needed to strengthen opportunities for linking individual change (in knowledge, attitudes and behaviours) with more systemic, culture change (in organizational norms and practices). Chapter 1 introduces the Gender at Work Analytical Framework, first developed in 2002 (see Rao and

Kelleher, 2005), which represents the evolution of this thinking about dimensions and pathways of change in support of gender equality. This tool is used throughout the book to help frame the analysis of GQAL strategies and outcomes.

In 1994, as we worked to develop the GQAL methodology, our key consideration was not only to increase the skills and knowledge of staff regarding gender, although, as noted above, we understood the importance of technical gender analysis and would ensure that any approach we used improved staff competency on gender analysis. In our conceptualization of organizational change, we also sought to bring to the fore the importance of supporting staff members through a process of learning that would build their individual consciousness of the 'value' of gender equality – in their day-to-day lives, their work and their interactions with others – as well as their capabilities to take 'action' to transform inequalities within the BRAC workplace and in BRAC programmes. This represented a departure from typical training approaches, with their careful division of public and private personas, emphasis on the development of professional or technical skills, and invisibilization of power and social positioning.

GQAL also highlighted problem-solving and problem-identification skills rather than offering pre-packaged 'solutions' for gender equality. The problem-identification process took GQAL participants into the murky world of social norms, bringing taken-for-granted assumptions about gender, status and power in the organization out into the open and inviting their collective interrogation. The team built GQAL around the belief that systemic change for gender equality required shifts in individuals' understanding, values and skills, and that these needed to be supported by an organizational culture that valued difference; that was inclusive and participatory; that valued experimentation and learning; and that was open to challenging patriarchal beliefs and ways of working. Trying to shift organizational thinking about what could be achieved using a different approach to 'training' was an initial challenge to overcome.

As the BRAC Gender Team, we knew that we needed senior managers' support for the GQAL initiative to get off the ground, but also that what we were proposing needed to push the envelope for change. The team believed that it was necessary to work with managers and staff to strengthen organizational systems, policies and procedures in support of BRAC's gender-equality goals. Also needed was leadership to support BRAC to develop an organizational culture that would allow it to attract and retain the best women and men and allow them to be their most productive selves. BRAC staff and managers were asked to identify (i.e., 'name') the dysfunctional cultural norms that shaped their behaviour and relationships, to question them, and to propose and practise new ways of working that could be supported by revised policies and re-engineered work systems. The team felt that this could be a promising foundation for sustainable organizational change. While we believed this approach was strategic, it was not always easy to convince key managers of its value.

As we explore in detail in the chapters of this book, GQAL supported staff members in BRAC to illuminate and make sense of organizational norms and practices, though this did not happen without resistance. This resistance, in turn, required creative strategies on the part of the GQAL Team. Through GQAL initiatives, staff were able to leverage policies and negotiate incentives structures in order to challenge an embedded patriarchal culture and promote gender equality. The value and importance of creating 'space' for staff members (and community members in later versions of GQAL) to surface and discuss gender and other inequalities, debate what underlies them and strategize how to change them are described in the chapters that follow as a key feature of the methodology, alongside the considerable challenges of implementing this ambitious, time-intensive approach to scale. The participatory, action-oriented approach was an innovation at the time (compared with more formulaic gender training), as was its emphasis on linking learning processes directly to organizational change (and not only to an increase in individual technical skills and knowledge). The lessons we have learned from GQAL, as we argue in the Conclusion, contribute to debates on how organizational change happens and how individual learning can influence and shape gender-equitable organizational change.

Another theme that emerges in telling the story of GQAL that is likely to be of relevance to wider debates on gender mainstreaming – particularly as a response to some of its detractors – is evidence of the relationship between internal organizational change efforts and changes in programme quality and outcomes. Evidence in support of GQAL's hypothesis that working for internal organizational change will have pay-offs in terms of improved outcomes for women and men in communities (a hypothesis that is shared by many efforts to mainstream gender) is offered throughout the book and explored again in the Conclusion.

Strategic choices and trade-offs

Those working to promote gender equality in organizations face a number of strategic choices related to the entry points that are prioritized and the extent to which social justice and human rights arguments are highlighted over more instrumental arguments about what women can contribute to other development (economic, health, social) outcomes. We could have used any number of different approaches to gender mainstreaming – for example, supporting BRAC to build gender policies and staff and programme-related gender accountability systems and/or focusing solely on building technical gender-analysis expertise among individual staff. However, for the reasons we describe above, we believed such strategies would be limited in their effectiveness.

As GQAL was designed and implemented, it became clear that internal organizational dynamics, often related to specific departments, created distinct incentive structures and ways of working that were, at times, inimical to gender equality and women's empowerment, and exerted influence despite the strong commitment from senior management. These dynamics meant that strategic choices had to be made by the GQAL Team about how gender issues and women's empowerment would be framed. The role of 'issue framing' and of discursive strategies in gender advocacy are now well acknowledged, as are the possible gains and likely trade-offs faced by gender advocates using language and arguments that are palatable to the different audiences they are trying to 'convince'.[9]

Within the organization, we needed to frame gender equality in a way that resonated with all staff. In addition to a wide range of attitudes to gender equality among BRAC staff (from commitment to ambivalence to opposition),[10] we were aware that the pre-eminence of micro-finance in BRAC's operations, with its emphasis on financial accountability, created some tensions within BRAC for improving its accountability on women's empowerment. As the GQAL manual (Stuart *et al.*, 1997) asks, 'How can the yin of women's empowerment live with the yang of credit?' These factors created challenges for the implementation of GQAL, and all against a backdrop of research suggesting that even a narrow interpretation of women's economic empowerment through access to credit was not necessarily improving women's ability to control the resources allocated to them. In the mid-1990s, BRAC was coming under scrutiny as research suggested male appropriation of loans and even that some women borrowers were experiencing increased violence from male relatives. Such research highlighted the need for micro-finance programmes to pay closer attention to intra-household gender relations and the complex interplay of conflict and co-operation that governs them (see, e.g., Goetz and Sen Gupta, 1996). GQAL attempted to navigate these tensions in part by emphasizing the 'Q' in GQAL – that is, 'quality' – and highlighting that paying attention to gender inequalities inside BRAC and in the communities where it works would improve its overall performance.

As we describe in this book, the GQAL design also prioritized the creation of space for staff (and, later, community members) to debate and define gender equality and women's empowerment based on their own experiences and problems. Sometimes, the analyses did not go as far as the team had hoped, but the importance of working with people where they were – and creating opportunities for self- and collective reflection on key gender-related issues – was central to our approach. Gendered power relations were brought to the surface and explored through GQAL. Especially in the earlier phases, power was often conceptualized using 'win–win' scenarios – that is, gender equality promoted healthy relations in the workplace or family harmony and well-being – rather than a 'zero-sum' game in which, for women to gain power, men had to lose power. Debates about women's empowerment (and what it means for men) have not yet been resolved,[11] though there is growing evidence to support the findings described in this book from both GQAL staff and GQAL in the community: namely, that when men respect women's rights, the quality of their own lives improves, too.

A strategic choice made by the GQAL Team from the beginning was to ensure that the process engaged both women and men staff (and, later, women and men community members) rather than working exclusively with women. This reflected our analysis that shifting gender power relations could not happen if we worked solely with women. As GQAL expanded to work in the community, this analysis played out at a different level in the strategic trade-offs that were made between mainstreaming GQAL into other BRAC programmes and developing stand-alone GQAL programming on gender equality.

Evolution, learning and adaptation

Since GQAL was introduced in BRAC in 1995, it has taken on a number of avatars, notably shifting from an internal focus on BRAC staff members to mainstreaming in major BRAC anti-poverty programming to a stand-alone programme in 2012 (see Appendix 1). Although BRAC has seen a number of other gender interventions prior and subsequent to GQAL, it remains seminal in terms of its influence across the organization. Over the 20 years since its inception, the manual *An Action-Learning Approach to Gender and Organizational Change* (Stuart *et al.*, 1997) has appeared front and centre on the Gender Justice and Diversity (GJD) Unit page on BRAC's website.[12]

Among other things, staff have referred to GQAL as 'training', as a 'programme', as a 'process' and as a 'team'. As we tell the story of GQAL and identify the threads that connect its various avatars, we also reflect on what its continuous evolution and reinvention have meant for BRAC and for strategizing for gender equality. In light of current thinking on 'adaptive development', we ask:

- What can we learn from GQAL as an approach that recognizes the complexity of social change processes and encourages – and, indeed, values – problem-solving and experimentation?
- What does this approach lend to learning about individual change, organizational change and norm change?
- What does the GQAL story tell us about the determination of BRAC gender staff to foster organizational change and community-level change in policies, resource access and social norms?
- What have we learned about the kinds of changes that are possible by taking this approach?

We situate these reflections in the context of developments that have occurred since 1994, such as the rise of the 'results'- and 'evidence'-based agendas, and the implications of measuring sometimes intangible results related to gender equality.

The structure of this book

The first chapter of this book sets the context in Bangladesh in 1994, at the beginning of the GQAL process, and outlines what BRAC was doing to promote gender equality at that time. This snapshot of BRAC is situated in the context of Bangladesh in the early 1990s.

The second chapter describes the origins of the GQAL process inside BRAC, the baseline study the GQAL Team undertook, and the process of designing and building agreement on the intervention. The third and fourth chapters describe two distinct phases of GQAL: the programme for BRAC staff; and the programme to implement GQAL in local communities, which began in 2001. These chapters describe the origins of these initiatives; how and why they changed over time; and the results of GQAL within BRAC and in the communities. While highlights of GQAL's role in local communities are described in some detail, we give greater emphasis to the initial phase of the programme implemented with BRAC staff, when central elements of the GQAL approach were conceptualized and tested. In so doing, we are able to provide a fuller description and examples of the GQAL methodology, in the hope that this will be of some interest to organizations seeking to try approaches other than standard gender training.

In the Conclusion, we explore the implications of learning from the GQAL Programme for the future, both for BRAC and for other organizations interested in promoting gender equality and social inclusion. This final chapter also situates GQAL's approach and impact within the context of current literature and debates on gender mainstreaming, gender and organizational change and gender-sensitive evaluation, including, as mentioned earlier in this chapter, thinking that is rooted in ideas of adaptive development.

Notes

1 Carol Miller was not directly involved in GQAL's work, but, as a practitioner and researcher on gender equality in development institutions over the past 25 years, she has collaborated as a 'critical friend' to support the writing of this book.
2 With accolades from leading figures such as Amartya Sen and Bill Gates, BRAC is well known and well respected for its work: see www.brac.net/#who_we_are BRAC. For more information on the organization's reach, see 'At a Glance, Global Headline Figures as of December 2015', www.brac.net/sites/default/files/ataglance/BRAC-at-a-glance-december-2015.pdf (accessed 7 November 2016).
3 For more information, see an overview of BRAC's goals related to gender equality: http://brac.net/gender-justice-diversity/item/843-overview (accessed 8 November 2016).
4 See http://brac.net/microfinance-programme/item/856-microfinance-for-women (accessed 8 November 2016).
5 See, for example, Acker (1990), Staudt (1990), Kardam (1991), Goetz (1992) and Jahan (1995).
6 For a fuller discussion of gender accountability and frustrations in NGOs in the 1990s, see Porter *et al.* (1999) on the experiences of gender staff at Oxfam, and Mayoux (1998) on gender accountability and NGOs.
7 Influenced by the ongoing work with BRAC, as well as the momentum post-Beijing around 'gender mainstreaming', three of this book's authors (Aruna Rao, Rieky Stuart and David Kelleher) organized a conference in Canada in 1996 to explore ways of merging thinking about gender equality and thinking about the

'deep structures' of organizations, from which was born both the book *Gender at Work: Organizational Change for Gender Equality* (1999) and, shortly thereafter, the organization Gender at Work. For more information about Gender at Work, see http://genderatwork.org/. In that book, we acknowledge that the work with BRAC gave us our first serious opportunity to explore the connections between gender and organizational change.

8 For more information, see http://genderatwork.org/OurWork/OurPrograms/Gen derActionLearningGAL.aspx.

9 See, for example, Razavi (1998) and 'Ruling out Gender Inequality: Why Good Policies Often Fail to be Implemented' in Rao *et al.* (2016), especially p. 109.

10 One unfounded critique of GQAL (Mannan, 2016) was that it replaced a locally designed, culturally appropriate gender-training programme. Mannan (2016) also argues that GQAL/gender equality initiatives were pushing ideas and values that were culturally inappropriate (i.e., 'Western') in BRAC and the communities that BRAC reached. This was not a critique that was ever levelled at the GQAL Programme from BRAC managers or staff at the time of its design and implementation. We tend to share the view put forward by Jolly in her research on gender and culture: 'Different people have different views about the cultures in which they live, and within any country or community there are many cultures. There is no homogenous fixed northern culture to impose on a homogenous and fixed southern culture' (Jolly, 2002: 2). What is more, people relate differently to the cultures in which they live. While some aspects of culture are enabling for some individuals, they can be constraining for others (Jolly, 2002: 2). As we explore throughout this book, GQAL, in all its phases, has attempted to create space for people to explore and challenge their assumptions about gender, gender equality and gender relations from their own perspectives and within specific contexts. It does not impose specific ideas about gender equality.

11 See Hughes *et al.* (2015) for a review of the current literature. See also Duncan Green's blog post (dated 27 August 2015) at https://oxfamblogs.org/fp2p/is-power-a-zero-sum-game-does-womens-empowerment-lead-to-increased-domestic-violence/.

12 At www.brac.net/gender.

References

Acker, J. (1990) 'Hierarches, Jobs, Bodies: A Theory of Gendered Organizations', *Gender and Society*, 4.2: 139–158.

Stuart, R., Rao, A., Kelleher, D., Hafiza, S., Sultana, N., Rahman, H., Rahman, S. (1997) *BRAC Technical Manual: An Action-Learning Approach to Gender and Organizational Change*, Dhaka: BRAC, www.brac.net/sites/default/files/BRAC-Technical-Manual-Chapter_01-07.pdf (accessed 2 March 2017).

Goetz, A.-M. (1992) 'Gender and Administration', *IDS Bulletin*, 23.4: 6–17.

Goetz, A.-M., Sen Gupta, R. (1996) 'Who Takes the Credit? Gender, Power, and Control over Loan Use in Rural Credit Programmes in Bangladesh', *World Development*, 24.1: 45–63.

Green, D. (2015) 'How Can Research Help Promote Empowerment and Accountability?' From Power to Poverty Blog, http://oxfamblogs.org/fp2p/how-can-research-help-us-promote-empowerment-and-accountability/ (accessed 2 March 2017).

Kabeer, N. (1994) *Reversed Realities: Gender Hierarchies in Development Thought*, London: Verso.

Kardam, N. (1991) *Bringing Women in: Women's Issues in International Development Programmes*, Boulder: Lynne Rienner.

Hughes, C., Bolis, M., Fries, R., Finigan, S. (2015) 'Women's Economic Inequality and Domestic Violence: Exploring the Links and Empowering Women', *Gender and Development*, 23.2: 279–297.

Jahan, R. (1995) *The Elusive Agenda: Mainstreaming Women in Development*, London: Zed.

Jolly, S. (2002) *Gender and Culture Change: Overview Report*, Brighton: Institute of Development Studies, www.bridge.ids.ac.uk/sites/bridge.ids.ac.uk/files/reports/CEP-culture-report.pdf (accessed 15 November 2016).

Kanter, R.M. (1977) *Men and Women of the Corporation*, New York: Basic Books.

Mannan, M. (2016) *BRAC, Global Policy Language, and Women in Bangladesh: Transformation and Manipulation*, Albany: SUNY Press.

March, C., Smyth, I., Mukhopadhyay, M. (1999) *A Guide to Gender-Analysis Frameworks*, Oxford: Oxfam.

Mayoux, L. (1998) 'Gender Accountability and NGOs: Avoiding the Black Hole' in C. Miller and S. Ravazi (eds), *Missionaries and Mandarins: Feminist Engagement with Development Institutions*, London: IT Publications.

Miller, C., Razavi, S. (1998a) *Gender Analysis: Alternative Paradigms, Gender in Development Monograph Series* No. 6, New York: UNDP.

Miller, C., Razavi, S. (eds) (1998b) *Missionaries and Mandarins: Feminist Engagement with Development Institutions*, London: IT Publications.

Molyneux, M. (1985) 'Mobilization without Emancipation? Women's Interests, State and Revolution in Nicaragua', *Feminist Studies*, 11.2: 227–254.

O'Neil, T. (2016) *Using Adaptive Development to Support Feminist Action*, London: ODI, www.odi.org/sites/odi.org.uk/files/resource-documents/10889.pdf (accessed 15 November 2016).

Pearson, R., Whitehead, A., Young, K. (1981) 'Introduction: The Continuing Subordination of Women in the Development Process' in C. Young, C. Wolkowitz and R. McCullagh (eds), *Of Marriage and Market*, London: CSE Books.

Porter, F., Smyth, I., Sweetman, C. (eds) (1999) *Gender Work: Oxfam Experience in Policy and Practice*, Oxford: Oxfam.

Rao, A., Feldstein, H., Cloud, K., Staudt, K. (1991) 'Introduction' in *Gender Training and Development Planning: Learning from Experience*, New York: The Population Council.

Rao, A., Kelleher, D. (2005) 'Is There Life after Gender Mainstreaming', *Gender and Development*, 13.2: 57–69.

Rao, A., Sandler, J., Kelleher, D., Miller, C. (2016) *Gender at Work: Theory and Practice for 21st Century Organizations*, Abingdon: Routledge.

Rao, A., Stuart, R., Kelleher, D. (1999) *Gender at Work: Organizational Change for Equality*, Hartford: Kumarian.

Razavi, S. (1998) 'Becoming Multilingual: The Challenges of Feminist Policy Advocacy' in C. Miller and S. Razavi (eds), *Missionaries and Mandarins: Feminist Engagement with Development Institutions*, London: IT Publications.

Razavi, S., Miller, C. (1995) *From WID to GAD: Conceptual Shifts in the Women and Development Discourse*, Geneva: UNRISD.

Staudt, K. (ed.) (1990) *Women, International Development, and Politics: The Bureaucratic Mire*, Philadelphia: Temple University Press.

1 The context in 1994

Although Bangladesh was known as a very poor country when we began this work in 1994, it has made substantial improvements in poverty reduction and human development. The World Bank, as of July 2015, labels Bangladesh as a 'lower middle income' country (it was previously ranked as a 'low income country').[1] According to the Human Development Index (HDI) 2015, 'Bangladesh's HDI value for 2014 is 0.570' – which puts the country in the medium human development category – positioning it at 142 out of 188 countries and territories.[2] Bangladesh has achieved significant improvements in the basic standard of living of its people. In 1994, it had a population of 115 million; it now has 159 million. GNP had risen from $350 per capita in 1994 to $750 per capita in constant dollars by 2014. While there has been some resistance from conservative Islamic individuals and groups, and considerable challenges for women remain, gender inequality in Bangladesh has decreased significantly in the past 20 years. The statistics in Table 1.1 present a remarkable story of change. Life expectancy has increased as well, and women, on average, now live two years longer than men; maternal mortality and infant mortality rates have been significantly lowered; and women are having far fewer children than in 1994. The job market for women has improved, as has their mobility; the garment sector, which accounts for more than 75 per cent of all export earnings, employs over 2 million women, most of whom are from rural areas.[3] But in 1994, the reins on women's lives were tighter and women had fewer options for mobility and voice.

Gender relations in Bangladesh in 1994[4]

In cultural terms, Bangladesh was and remains a relatively homogeneous society: in 1994, 90 per cent of the population was Muslim and 98 per cent of the population spoke Bengali (Blanchet, 1986).

Like its South Asian counterparts, Bangladesh was and is a highly patriarchal society. Within the household and through local decision-making and legal bodies like the *shamaj* (neighbourhood associations) and *salish* (local dispute resolution bodies), men exercised control over women's labour, sexuality, choice of marriage partner, access to markets, and income and assets. Men

Table 1.1 Comparison of gender statistics in Bangladesh 1994 and 2014

	1994		2014★	
GDP per person (in constant dollars)	$350		$750	
Fertility rate	4.7		2.21	
Maternal mortality rate	6/1000		2.2/1000	
	M	F	M	F
Literacy rate	47%	22%	64%[†]	56%[†]
Gross enrolment in primary school	83%	71%	98%	98.4%
Gross enrolment in secondary school	25%	12%	50%	57%
Gross enrolment in tertiary education	5.9%	1.3%	11%	15%
Life expectancy	55.9	54.4	69.9	71.5
Labour force participation rate	87%	16%	88%	58%
Share of employment in agricultural activity	49%	51%		
Share of employment in non-agricultural activity	85%	15%		
Proportion of paid workers earning more than 300 taka/week (1994)	61.7%	19%		
Share of unpaid family labour	26%	74%	26%[‡]	74%[‡]
Political representation			82%	18%
Employment in civil service	94%	6%	89%	11%[†]

Sources: ★ Data from Bangladesh Bureau of Statistics, World Bank, UN agencies; [‡] Data from Centre for Policy Dialogue (CPD) and Manusher Jonno Foundation (MJF), cited in Benar News, 1 October 2015.

Notes: Wherever possible, figures are from 2014; [†] Most recent data is from 2012 or 2013.

mediated women's access to social, economic, political and legal institutions. Women were dependent on men throughout their lives, from fathers through husbands to sons. State legislation and institutions served to reinforce this gender subordination and relationship of dependence, in spite of constitutional affirmations of equality between women and men. Men's authority over women was also reinforced by pervasive gender-based violence. In 1993, Bangladesh experienced an increase in such violence from Islamic fundamentalists, expressed through actions such as burning schools, cutting down the mulberry trees women needed to feed silkworms, and attacking local NGOs perceived to be fronts for Christian proselytizing.

At the time, women operated within a rigid gender division of labour. Purdah norms had been challenged after the War of Liberation, when millions of women were forced to seek work outside the home to survive. Nevertheless, some aspects of purdah survived. The Islamic social institution of purdah defined separate spaces for men and women and tied the protection of family honour (*izzat*) to the control of female sexuality. It restricted women's mobility outside the homestead and thus their ability to participate in a range of economic activities and in local governance and decision-making. Through purdah, male relatives controlled the private sphere and male authorities controlled the public sphere. Purdah was the means by which a rigid functional and spatial gender division of labour was upheld, norms regarding appropriate behaviours were internalized, and women's subjugation was formalized in law and custom (Adnan, 1989).

As a result, the disparity in completion rates between girls' and boys' education was among the highest in the world. Bangladesh was also one of few countries where the ratio of women to men was below the global average, indicating that significant numbers of women were dying from female infanticide, malnutrition, spousal violence and/or lack of access to healthcare. Physical violence against women was common in about 90 per cent of all households, and both men and women agreed that beating one's wife was justified.[5]

Nevertheless, there had been some progress since independence in 1975. Immunization and life expectancy had risen significantly and fertility rates were falling. Increasingly, women were gaining access to credit, education and jobs, as well as organizing to fight for their legal rights. Government policies to facilitate girls' education, such as free education and stipends for attending school, were being developed and were pivotal to increasing girls' secondary school attendance. Among those programmes, free textbooks, food for education, community satellite schools and improving water and sanitation facilities in the schools were all noteworthy.

As elsewhere in the world, women's experiences and interests were strongly defined by their class position. Increasing pauperization and landlessness propelled some poorer rural women into activities to increase household incomes. However, given a large surplus of unemployed and underemployed rural labour, discriminatory and segmented labour markets, and the fact that most rural women were uneducated and unskilled, such women were highly disadvantaged vis-à-vis their male counterparts in seeking employment outside the home. Women in better-off, landowning households were less likely to engage in outside work because this labour indicated poverty and lower social status.

Similarly, women's political participation was limited, though parliamentary seats had been reserved for women since independence. In the 5th Parliament (1991–1995), for example, there were 30 seats reserved and 34 women MPs (less than 10 per cent of all parliamentarians). And although two women had served as Prime Minister and Leader of the Opposition since 1991, their prominent presence was anomalous and belied the marginal position of most women in Bangladeshi politics (Jalal, n.d.).

In 1994, women's employment opportunities outside the homestead were limited. Organized food for work and other employment schemes provided some employment for impoverished rural women, but these were limited in both scope and duration. In some areas, landless women collectively leased government-owned land or ponds (*'khas'*) to engage in activities such as live-stock and poultry rearing, vegetable production and fishpond cultivation (Jahan, 1989). Some younger women with a formal education were starting to find employment in non-traditional spheres such as education, health and family planning, and extension work related to rural development (Eggen, 1988).

The lack of employment opportunities in rural areas also triggered increasing rural–urban migration, including of female-headed households. Migrant women found employment in domestic service, a variety of informal sector occupations (including prostitution), and casual unskilled labour, such as in the construction industry. Some younger women in urban and semi-urban areas were taking up factory employment in export-oriented industries such as garments, where the labour force was predominantly female (Eggen, 1988). Other manufacturing sectors, such as shrimp processing, leather goods manu-facture and toy manufacture had the potential to employ significant numbers of women, but in 1994 most of those in manufacturing still worked in cottage industries as unpaid family labourers.

BRAC's early days

BRAC started in 1972 as a relief and rehabilitation organization, following a fierce struggle for independence from Pakistan in 1971. The relief work was initiated by a few young, altruistic, highly educated men committed to serve millions of war-affected people returning from refugee camps in India, where they had fled during the fighting. Upon realizing after a year that relief was important but insufficient, BRAC changed its focus to development in order to contribute to building Bangladesh through poverty alleviation and empower-ment. The work culture of BRAC, however, remained very masculine, in keeping with wider social norms and practices; working hours were long and continued far into the night, and the work involved difficult travel to remote villages with very poor roads and very little communications infrastructure. BRAC's work in rural areas was novel in Bangladesh at that time. Not only were living and working conditions hard, but collegial and family relationships took a back seat to work. Staff who asked for leave, even for the birth of a child or family illness, were perceived as less committed to BRAC's goals than those who made work their only priority.

The female staff of BRAC in the 1980s were often the first women in their community to take public transport, follow post-secondary-level studies in cities and/or work in an office. It was not socially acceptable for them to work in the way BRAC required – as staff posted to area offices in rural areas who lived and worked in compounds with men who were not relatives. BRAC helped women staff in some ways – for example, by offering them modest residential facilities in a few places. The Health Programme (WHDP) offices were smaller than the Rural Development Programme (RDP) offices, with only 10–12 staff, the majority of whom were women who often worked with only one male programme organizer or area manager. The RDP offices, in contrast, were predominantly staffed by men.

What BRAC was like in 1994[6]

By 1994, BRAC had approximately 15,000 staff serving 1.6 million village-based members, grouped into 'Village Organizations' (VOs). This made it the world's largest indigenous not-for-profit development organization, with the twin goals of poverty alleviation and empowerment of the poor.

BRAC's work in communities was organized by its Area Offices, which were home to multiple programmes, including those offering micro-credit and health services. The Area Managers were, in turn, grouped into regions supervised by Regional Managers.

BRAC's history reflected a set of strategic learning points along with important policy and programming shifts. From the initial focus in 1972 on relief and rehabilitation – necessitated, in large part, by devastating monsoon floods following the end of the war of independence – the organization took on a community development approach to poverty alleviation. By the early 1990s, BRAC had graduated to a target-oriented approach to sustainable development and empowerment, delivering micro-credit primarily to poor women, in addition to basic healthcare and primary education.

BRAC had also taken on a host of supplementary services, ranging from income-generation skills training, human rights and legal education, a family planning and women's health programme, to non-formal education of BRAC members' children, and higher-order economic enterprises to market the products produced by BRAC members, like Aarong and BRAC Cold Storage.[7] These enterprises made a significant contribution to the local economy by creating market linkages and employment opportunities and supporting entrepreneurs. By targeting profitable and scalable businesses, BRAC enterprises were able to fulfil their social missions on a much greater scale, while the profits they earned supported BRAC's development programmes and other innovations.

While not every sub-district offered every programme, by 1994 BRAC was well aware that poverty was more complex than the absence of money, and needed to be tackled in a holistic way. Moreover, BRAC's leadership recognized that there needed to be clear goalposts, such as performance targets, in BRAC programming.

Over the last 20 years, BRAC's size and portfolio have increased exponentially (see Table 1.2). Micro-finance, education and health remain the most important programmes, just as they were in 1994, absorbing approximately 70 per cent of overall development spending, although their scope and resources are more extensive than before. Staff are no longer required to live

Table 1.2 Comparison of BRAC in 1994 and 2014

	1994	2014
Number of beneficiaries reached	1,600,000 borrowers	4,000,000 micro-finance borrowers *Programme beneficiaries:*
		25,000,000 (MNCH) 3,700,000 (HRLS) 2,200,000 (Gender) 700,000 (Education) 500,000 (Migration) 60,000 (Agriculture) 950,000 (Community empowerment)
Number of staff	15,000 (3,000 – 20% – women)	42,826 (10,594 – 25% – women) *Distribution of female staff:*
		Front line (20% of staff total): 62% women Mid-level (4% of staff total): 14% women Senior staff (1% of staff total): 24% women
Budget	$71,000,000	$845,000,000
Social enterprises	4 companies (Aarong, BRAC Garments, BRAC Printers, Cold Storage)	17 companies
Other initiatives	Ayesha Abed Foundation	Ayesha Abed Foundation BRAC Bank BRAC International BRAC University

together 'on campus' at the Area Office, as transport is better and rental accommodation is more available. BRAC has a wide range of social enterprises, such the BRAC Feed Mills, which were developed to provide inputs and marketing services for BRAC clients and to sustain a range of other development programmes. In the years since 1994, BRAC has also replicated its approach to poverty alleviation in several Asian and African countries under the leadership of BRAC International.

Characteristics of BRAC's culture and programming

Innovation and learning for results

From the early days, BRAC's goal of poverty reduction was translated into clear and measurable results for staff. A good example of this results-based programming is the Oral (Rehydration) Therapy Extension Programme (OTEP).

Diarrhoea was a major killer of children until American and Bengali doctors developed a simple salt/sugar/water treatment in the late 1960s that the *Lancet* called 'potentially the most important medical advance of the 20th century'.[8] Learning how to disseminate its lifesaving formula in poor communities was a challenge that BRAC addressed through OTEP. BRAC 'barefoot' health workers were trained to teach village women oral rehydration therapy to treat children with diarrhoea. They were paid not according to how many women they instructed, but how well the mothers could recall the instructions and accurately prepare and administer the salt/sugar/water solution to their children. Monitors also checked whether women were successful in treating diarrhoea and, if not, identified barriers that needed to be addressed. BRAC's success in disseminating the knowledge and skills to treat diarrhoea using this model has meant that diarrheal disease is now responsible for 2 per cent of all deaths in children under five in Bangladesh, compared to 20 per cent 30 years ago.

OTEP was unique in that it was the first programme to employ rural women and sanction their mobility, because this was essential for the programme's success. It was also interesting because, in monitoring uptake, BRAC discovered that village mothers needed their husbands' and mothers-in-law's permission to use the treatment. In response to this information, BRAC extended its outreach to include men, although it did not include an effort to increase women's say in this matter.

This same rigorous experimentation in establishing and monitoring specific outcome-level targets and figuring out how to achieve them, which existed for each programme in 1994, continues today. It is an important factor in BRAC's success.

Going to scale

Taking its innovations to scale – reaching millions, not hundreds – is another hallmark of BRAC's culture. BRAC's founder, Sir F.H. Abed, summed up this approach by saying that 'small is beautiful, but large is necessary'. What this means is that each programme consists of clearly articulated steps and measures that can be accomplished by field-level workers and their clients, and can be made highly efficient, not unlike the design of manufacturing processes. So, if poor women took loans to raise chicks for income and food for their families, there needed to be timely transport for the chicks, appropriate chicken feed, 'barefoot' veterinarians to inoculate the chickens, and, as production rose, accessible slaughtering, processing and marketing facilities. Figure 1.1 schematically illustrates BRAC's approach to piloting, experimentation and scaling up its programmes.

Belonging to the BRAC family

An important thread of BRAC's culture was the sense of belonging to a family: the founding BRAC staff became very close, a common phenomenon among people who share an intense experience. Their long hours and dedication to work were a source of pride and fostered a sense of belonging. BRAC was

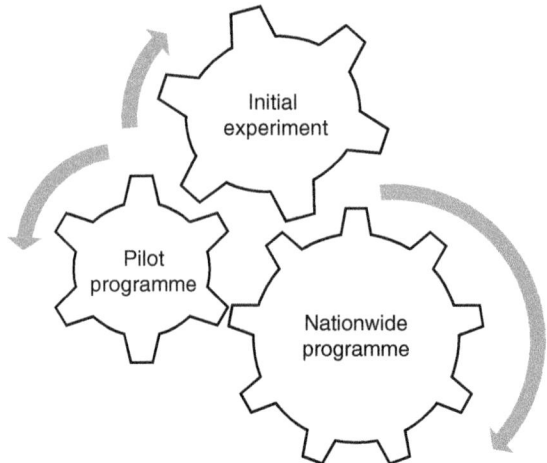

Figure 1.1 BRAC's response to emerging challenges in Bangladesh
Note: This figure is inspired by K. Bakker, BRAC intern and SIT student.

dedicated to delivering quality services, and sacrifice was seen as part of this culture. This thread of mutual support and accountability was becoming increasingly frayed, however, as BRAC's staff grew from hundreds to thousands and then over 10,000 in the 1990s, and as young idealists became parents with increased family responsibilities.

Work–family balance was a big issue for women and men. Field offices were in remote areas and staff were often deployed far from their homes. They were expected not to take leave even during family emergencies or, for male staff, even as their wives were giving birth. Expressions of family concerns were viewed as signs of weakness.

Social pioneering

Another aspect of BRAC's culture was the desire to be 'social pioneers', modelling integrity, hard work and the respectful behaviour that were seen as essential to achieving BRAC's mandate. BRAC was, and remains, a complex organization with an internal culture forged both in contestation and in compliance with its surrounding culture. As noted above, BRAC was formed to alleviate the poverty and misery prevalent in Bangladesh after its war of independence. The culture of successful resistance – which extracted a heavy toll of death and suffering for its citizens, and was still a powerful memory in the 1990s – built upon the fact that many of BRAC's staff had either fought or fled in the civil war. This thread of successful resistance became ingrained in the 'social pioneering' culture of BRAC. It remains today in the pride of BRAC staff who can see evidence of healthier, more prosperous and better-educated recipients of BRAC services and programmes. This attitude is often cited in staff evaluations. Yet modelling norms that were not widely accepted also took a toll on BRAC staff, and the price was often higher for women who contravened accepted practice than for men, as illustrated in the story that appears in the box.

> Before the beginning of the GQAL programme, one of the female Programme Officers assigned to collect loans with micro-finance colleagues cycled ten kilometres to a neighbouring village for this purpose. She was still nursing her 11-month-old child, and became extremely uncomfortable and distressed as the hours passed and her colleagues, who were all bachelors, were in no hurry to return, despite her urging. Finally, after midnight, she broke down in tears of pain and distress, and one of her colleagues cycled back with her. Her husband, distraught and angry, locked her out of the house until she promised to quit her job. Only her Regional Manager's intervention to forbid women to do field work at night persuaded her husband to relent, after much discussion between him and her colleagues. This woman said such conditions would be unimaginable for BRAC staff today.
>
> (Staff interviews, 2015)

Culture of fear

Alongside the culture of belonging to the BRAC family was what some staff referred to as a 'culture of fear' – a fear of making mistakes, of impossibly high performance targets, and of abuse of power among managers. Staff did exactly, and only, as they were told. This culture of fear, in turn, encouraged staff to hide or deny problems and generated a 'culture of shifting responsibility' – in other words, it was the deliveryman's fault, or the weather's fault, or the borrower's fault, or the manager's fault if the chicks died, not the fault of the Programme Officer (Ghuznavi, 2008).

Culture of silence

In 1994 there was very little public discourse about issues facing women staff in BRAC: sexual harassment, physical and sexual violence, reproductive health and bodily functions were all taboo topics even among women, and much more so between women and men. The Women's Advisory Committee (WAC), set up in 1991 by the Executive Director and described in more detail below, began talking in 1993 about menstruation and restrictions on women's mobility, but sexual harassment was not raised publicly within the organization until 1997.

Instead, women experienced these issues and suffered in silence or, at best, in whispered conversations among close confidantes. This silence made it difficult to raise the profile of such issues or establish the scope of the problem, let alone take steps to address harassment. In this respect, BRAC's culture in 1994 followed, rather than challenged, societal standards. Steven Lukes' (2006) insightful analysis of power tells us that the ability to define topics that cannot be discussed is an important dimension of power; this is nowhere more evident than in the silence regarding sexual harassment and violence in BRAC, which enabled and perpetuated gender inequality.

The Women's Action Committee and the first gender training course in BRAC provided opportunities for those individuals who were courageous enough to share their experiences to begin publicizing the scope and size of the issues facing BRAC women staff and the women clients with whom they worked. But the senior BRAC women managers on the WAC had no formal mechanisms with which systematically to raise or address the problems raised. Often, both women and men colleagues found it embarrassing to discuss such issues. Examples of the inequitable practices that surfaced in discussions and how addressing them came to be part of the BRAC agenda are described throughout this book.

Subordinate role of women

In the mid-1990s, BRAC male staff and mid-level managers were reluctant to hire women because they felt that they could not cope with the conditions in rural communities and Area Offices, and that they were incapable of fulfilling the tasks required by their job descriptions (Ghuznavi, 2008). Women staff were often asked to serve tea to guests and take care of other 'housekeeping' duties. They seldom spoke up at staff meetings and, like their male counterparts, were not consulted about the agendas for staff meetings by managers. Working hours were long, and often extended into late evenings when credit collections had to be counted and registered, and reports were due. Male staff said they would not recommend BRAC as an employer for female family members.

Transfers were common for both women and men staff. Some supervisors shouted and threw papers at their staff, and people who objected were transferred. While these stories were not true for all BRAC Area Offices, and probably not even the majority, they accurately portray an organizational culture where women's contributions were not valued: not one respondent in the research undertaken for this book mentioned that women were better able to interact and establish rapport with village women, even though official BRAC publications, and senior managers, lauded the work of 'volunteer' women health workers – women who were not official members of staff but achieved remarkable results.

These hallmarks of BRAC culture did not sit easily together, particularly in the period of rapid expansion that marked BRAC in the early 1990s. Being 'head of the family' of a BRAC programme became challenging when staff numbered in the thousands, rather than the hundreds. For a local programme assistant, taking time to listen to and interact with clients might mean falling short on loan disbursement and collection schedules. Staff tended to focus only on their own roles in the process, particularly because the tasks were so specifically articulated and their efficiency in carrying them out was monitored. There was high staff turnover and an attitude that those who did not thrive in this culture were probably not capable. Though failed recruitments were costly in terms of staff time, staff were frequently dismissed or encouraged to resign.

Infrastructure and BRAC culture

The majority of BRAC staff was based in Area Offices, the main unit of BRAC's service delivery. Each Area Office was housed in a large (by village standards) compound and included living quarters for staff, since rental accommodation was hard to come by in villages. The BRAC staff often included cooks and cleaners. The office was the base from which staff departed to meet with BRAC clients to offer services and advice, as well as collect loan repayments and fees. The Rural Development Programme (which provided micro-credit and income-generating support services of various kinds) was the largest programme, so it had the most Area Offices. The Health Programme also had many Area Offices, but the Primary Education Programme, which hired and trained educated village women as teachers, did not need such an extensive outreach structure.

Private rooms and washing and toilet facilities that allowed privacy for both women and men were not guaranteed. Sometimes women were crowded together in one or two rooms; sometimes there were no facilities for family members who came to visit; and there was no guarantee of fair access for both women and men to the 'best' and the 'worst' the offices had to offer. Standards differed among the offices. Married women faced particular tensions and stress because they were separated from their families. In 1993, only about 25 per cent of married women Programme Officers and Area Managers lived with their spouses and children, compared to 50 per cent of men (Goetz, 1997: 21).[9]

At the time, BRAC was growing so fast that newly hired staff received very little initial support. If they stayed on the job after their immersion in field offices, new staff would receive training. This was possible because universities were generating large numbers of graduates who were competing for jobs, and the first months of work in a field office became, in essence, part of the self-selection process. The pressure-filled early period was particularly acute for women, who often faced strong pressure from their families to marry or not to live 'unsupervised' in the BRAC offices, in addition to the stress of learning a challenging new job and acting as a role model for others in the community. As noted above, BRAC staff were encouraged to think of themselves as 'social pioneers', modelling the behaviours and attitudes that they hoped to promote: mutual respect, cooperation, honesty and hard work.

Bicycle or motorbike riding was mandatory for all BRAC's field staff; otherwise mobilization, monitoring and supervision of programmes was impossible. Roads were poor and ill suited to any kind of local transport, and walking was out of the question as distances were large. But because it was not socially acceptable for women to ride bikes or motorbikes, local men and boys might shout at them, throw stones, or try to cause their bikes to overturn. When they travelled, women staff suffered, especially during their menstrual period, due to a lack of usable toilet facilities in villages. They often developed urinary tract infections or suffered from dehydration as they avoided drinking water during the working day for fear of incontinence. Pregnancy posed an additional challenge, as talking and informing others about early pregnancy was taboo, and if a miscarriage occurred during field visits, it could be catastrophic.

Management oversight

Another underpinning of BRAC's culture was field visits by regional and Head Office staff. These were seen as important ways for managers to understand what was happening in the rural areas, and to identify and solve problems. It was a regular practice of the Head Office's mid- to senior-level managers to go on field visits on Thursday and spend the weekend (Friday and Saturday) at field offices working with local staff, returning on Sunday to start the working week back at their own offices. This meant that, in effect, they had no days off, and nor did the staff in the Area Offices they visited. This is another example of how staff were expected to have no family responsibilities and, indeed, to be continuously available to their supervisors and clients.

Targets

When we visited Area Offices in 1994, we were struck that every office had the same chart on the wall. It carefully noted loan disbursements and repayments. We later learned that meeting targets was a key, defining characteristic of the job of Programme Officer (PO). POs were assessed largely on their capacity to meet targets (Rao et al., 1999). Nazneen (2007) describes conversations in which BRAC field staff recounted how, between loan disbursement, collection and report writing, they simply did not have the time for other considerations, such as intervening in a family where a woman faced violence. They were very clear that they would be 'scolded' – or worse – if they did not meet their targets.

The gendered dimensions of BRAC's culture, as well as their structural underpinnings, have changed significantly over time, in no small measure as a result of GQAL.

What BRAC was doing to promote gender equality in 1994

BRAC's work in communities

At this time in BRAC's history, it was providing services mostly to women. Like other micro-credit organizations in Bangladesh, BRAC's main targets for loans were women, organized in village-level borrower groups called VOs (Village Organizations) comprising 30 to 40 members. There were men bor- rowers, but 85 per cent of all credit was targeted at women. BRAC also had a Non-Formal Education Programme (NFEP) with over 35,000 schools. Seventy per cent of the students were girls. BRAC also had a Maternal Health Pro- gramme and a Para-Legal Programme, which trained women in basic aspects of family law and raised their awareness of their rights.

However, in the early 1990s, research was beginning to show that while increased income helped the family, in some cases women and girls derived little benefit from their loans or suffered if their enterprises failed and they still had to repay the loans (Goetz and Sen Gupta, 1996). BRAC's leadership was aware of this research and wanted to address this challenge.[10]

Inside BRAC

In the 1990s, BRAC underwent a tremendous expansion in area coverage and increased its staff strength. In the late 1980s, fuelled by its Executive Director's growing commitment to gender equality – a direction that had been encouraged over time by donors and numerous evaluation and appraisal missions – BRAC began actively recruiting and fast-tracking female staff. In 1994, approximately 20 per cent of all regular BRAC staff were women (this excluded its primary school teachers, who were mainly part-time, contract female staff). Women staff were largely concentrated in the Health Programme and the Head Office. A minority were in the RDP. In Bangladesh, given the country's strict gender norms, it was much easier for women staff to interact with women clients.

BRAC's expansion, together with its interest in recruiting more women staff and its commitment to women's empowerment, posed considerable challenges both organizationally and programmatically. Over the preceding three years, BRAC had adopted incremental policy changes in response to specific issues raised by women staff. This model had to be adapted to suit the growing organization.

In 1991, the Executive Director, who was concerned with attracting and retaining more women, appointed a Women's Advisory Committee. This was made up of senior women who were tasked with advising the organization on issues that were pertinent to women staff. Their first step was to organize a consultation with a nationally known expert on how to make BRAC a 'women-friendly organization'. The committee travelled to Area Offices and met with women staff. They would report their findings to the Executive Director and Programme Chiefs.

Around this time, four of BRAC's 20 senior managers were women, the number of female Area Managers was growing, and there was 'fast-track' pro- motion to increase the number of women staff overall. Later, in 1995, BRAC announced a policy of all-women recruitment. Although this was discontinued the following year, it sent a clear signal that the organization was prioritizing the recruitment and advancement of women staff.

While consulting with women staff, WAC heard complaints of sexual harassment and other types of discriminatory behaviour toward women. The committee felt that more intensive efforts to combat discrimination were needed, and its work resulted in some significant policy changes. For example, BRAC instituted a policy of 'desk work' for women staff who were menstruating so as to avoid long bicycle rides and sanitary issues in villages, although some women staff reported that they were either too embarrassed to take advantage of the policy unless they had a female manager or declined the offer of desk leave because they did not want their male colleagues to feel they were shirking their duties (Goetz, 1997: 24). In 1992, BRAC issued a circular on Community Living in response to some of the gender-related problems relating to women and men living and working together in close quarters. For example, the circular stipulated that women and men must not enter one another's rooms, and it stressed the importance of respectful behaviour between the sexes (Goetz, 1997: 19). The WAC also recommended the launch of a training course called 'Men and Women: Partnership in Development'. This module was intended to be a day-long session appended to all existing BRAC training courses. However, course leaders subsequently shortened it to half a day and, later, to just one hour.

In 1993, senior managers held a consultation to understand 'the gender question'. They heard recommendations from the Women's Action Committee and assessed the need for gender training for staff. As result, in July 1993, BRAC piloted its first comprehensive, all-staff gender-training programme, the Gender Awareness and Analysis Course (GAAC). This was the first such course targeted at NGO staff in Bangladesh, and it is still offered within BRAC as well as to leaders of other national and international organizations and government officials. The five-day course aimed to familiarize staff with global development trends and concepts of 'gender' and 'gender analysis', and to support staff to identify programmatic priorities in relation to changing the condition and status of women. The intent was to build capacity among BRAC staff by raising their gender awareness and developing their gender analysis skills so that they would be better equipped to facilitate empowerment at the grass roots with programme participants.

While the course was well received initially, its emphasis was conceptual more than applied, and there was no follow-up to determine whether attitudes and behaviour had changed. The trainers who developed the course, as well as some senior managers, felt more was needed: BRAC wanted to review the course and take it to a higher level. Earlier, F.H. Abed, BRAC's Executive Director, had heard Dr Aruna Rao deliver a gender training programme in Nepal using the case method.[11] Abed wanted Rao to launch a similar programme for BRAC, but she replied that training was not enough: addressing institutional factors was equally important. Her response provided the impulse for convening what became the GQAL Team.

The Gender at Work Analytical Framework

The foregoing discussion presents a complex picture of programmes, services, cultures, organizational norms and good intentions. In order to understand this, during and following our work with BRAC, we struggled to develop a way of thinking that could help us negotiate the complex terrain of change that included a concern for individual mindsets and social norms while pursuing systemic and policy changes. The result was the Gender at Work Analytical Framework (Rao et al., 2016).

What evolved from reflection and discussion at a series of conferences and kitchen-table conversations was a conception of change that is multi-factorial and holistic. It was concerned with the individual psychology of women and men, their access to resources, and an examination of the social structures in which they live. Furthermore, our conception was intervention focused: its starting point was an attempt to change the norms and structures underlying inequality. Our understanding was that change must happen in many places. It needs to affect individuals and the communities and organizations of which they are members, to shift norms and capabilities as well as improve access to resources. These dimensions were combined in the framework shown in Figure 1.2.

The top two quadrants are individual. On the right are changes in observable individual conditions, such as increased resources, voice, freedom from violence, access to health and education. On the left, we map individual consciousness and capability in the form of knowledge, skills, political consciousness, and commitment to change and build cultures of equality.

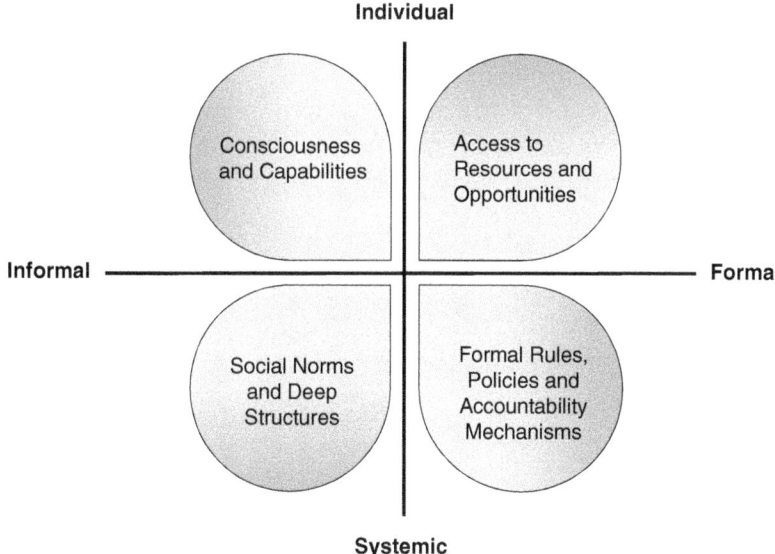

Figure 1.2 Gender at Work Analytical Framework

The bottom two quadrants are systemic. The quadrant on the right refers to formal rules as laid down in policies and organizational regulations. The quadrant on the left represents informal norms and practices, including those that maintain inequality in everyday practices.

Quadrant I: Individual consciousness and capabilities

This quadrant asks us about the individuals in the organization, community or society. Are they aware of their rights? Do they value gender equality and are they willing and able to take action to make their society more gender equitable? Change in this quadrant often results in a transformation of an individual's understanding of her own identity. Women no longer see themselves as victims of an unmovable system but as actors and activists who have agency. Through their own actions, they can challenge and change critical aspects of their situation.

If we were looking at this quadrant in an organizational analysis, we would be similarly focused on the consciousness and capabilities of organizational members and leaders and their willingness to take action.

Quadrant II: Resources

The top right-hand quadrant is about resources. In the community context, resources are such assets as women's access to micro-credit, health and education, or less tangible essentials like personal security and freedom from violence. This quadrant has received the bulk of attention from development agencies over the years. There is no doubt that this attention is valuable, and there have been impressive gains in such areas as girls' access to primary education and women's access to primary healthcare.

In an organizational analysis we would be looking at the resources available for work on gender equality, such as access to leadership, financial resources and mechanisms of protection against sexual harassment and violence.

As important as resources are, for both communities and organizations, increased resources may have a limited impact on women's capacity to change or challenge institutional norms regarding their position in society. For example, many micro-credit programmes were aimed at poverty alleviation but left gender relations largely intact (Goetz and Sen Gupta, 1996).

Quadrant III: The rules

The bottom right-hand quadrant is the region of formal policies, rules or arrangements. Within organizations, we look at whether there are policies and rules that will advance gender equality or whether the existing rules are gender discriminatory and need to be changed. For example, through the

1990s, BRAC implemented a variety of gender-friendly policies. Examples included a gender-equality policy, desk leave, extended maternal leave and paternal leave.

Quadrant IV: Social norms and deep structure

The bottom left-hand quadrant is about social norms and the deep structures in which inequalities are embedded (Rao and Kelleher, 2002). Because gender carries such strong implications for power and identity, the deep structure is a pattern of the deepest-held, stated and unstated norms and practices that govern gender relations. These norms are often invisible because they are so normalized. For example, when we first worked in Bangladesh, no one questioned that only men go to the markets. Even now, in many parts of the world, most people do not notice or challenge traditional gender roles or divisions of labour.

When we look at organizations, we examine how the 'normal' way of doing things affects women's power and the ability to make a full contribution to the organization.

In working with norms and deep structures, our concern is first to analyse how ideology and social norms and practices prescribe fixed gender roles, limit women's opportunities to exercise their rights, limit interventions for change, and often override or circumvent formal laws or constitutions that mandate equality.

The benefit of a framework such as the Gender at Work Analytic Framework is that it draws distinctions and creates analytic categories. It allows us to differentiate types of change. While this exercise is very helpful, the structure of the Framework can also obscure the links between the quadrants. In fact, the boundaries between the quadrants are porous, and change in one quadrant can have important ripple effects in the others.

A gender analysis of BRAC in 1994

Using the Framework described above, we can see that BRAC's major contribution to gender equality was the provision of resources that are intended to alleviate poverty and empower women. In its work in communities, the assumption was that, by earning an income, women would have more influence in household decision-making and would be able to: accumulate small amounts of capital; associate more freely with other women; and learn about their individual and collective rights. Within the organization, BRAC was also starting to provide increased resources for women staff by fast-tracking them to management positions and trying to alleviate some of the more challenging aspects of life in Area Offices. BRAC was also beginning to give women staff a voice through the WAC.

Regarding the bottom quadrant, BRAC started to put formal mechanisms in place to support gender equality. Among these were the WAC, the GAAC and the desk leave policy. However, there were no policies or mechanisms in place to support work–life balance and family leave, or to address sexual harassment and other instances of gender discrimination.

On the top-left side of the matrix – Consciousness and Capabilities – we see the beginning of efforts to understand gender dynamics and promote gender equality. These efforts are reflected in the GAAC, and in a commitment on the part of some managers, particularly the Executive Director, to advance gender equality. However, for many staff who lacked gender training and/or an independent commitment to gender equality, this was *terra incognita*.

It is in looking at social norms that we see the magnitude of the problem in BRAC. The social norms of rural Bangladesh were far from supportive of women working outside the home, meeting men who were not their relatives (i.e., programme staff) and having any say in the use of household income. There was also considerable opposition from fundamentalist groups who saw BRAC as leading communities away from Islam.

Although BRAC may have been falling short of many feminist ideas of empowerment (see Chapter 2), its leadership was (carefully) challenging important gender norms in communities, for example by having male Programme Officers talk with female villagers in the absence of male relatives; BRAC female staff live with male staff in Area Offices; and women staff ride bicycles and motorbikes. All of these activities were deeply countercultural. At the same time, BRAC had its own normative problems. Area Offices exemplified a masculine culture that valued hard work and long hours, unencumbered by family responsibilities. Typically, field staff held traditional ideas about women. Moreover, the intense focus on achieving programmatic targets made other considerations difficult to entertain. Looking back, the Director of Gender Justice and Diversity summed up the situation as follows:

> [B]efore the GQAL programme, the values that shaped both the broader social context and the BRAC environment produced programmes designed to change women's socioeconomic condition with little or no emphasis on changing gender power relations. Many gender issues weren't recognized. A BRAC Programme Assistant said, 'I joined BRAC just before GQAL started. My colleague used to discourage me to work and suggested I should leave the office and go home. [He said] women are fit only for household work. However, now things have changed.'
>
> (Hafiza, 2013: 1)

The team's gender analysis of BRAC is summarized in Figure 1.3.

Of course, no one had this clear a picture at the time, but BRAC's management wanted to do more to address gender inequality. Its leaders invited an external team, led by Dr Aruna Rao, to work with its Training Division to intensify BRAC's efforts on gender equality in a manner that would reach huge numbers of staff, influencing their attitudes and behaviour.

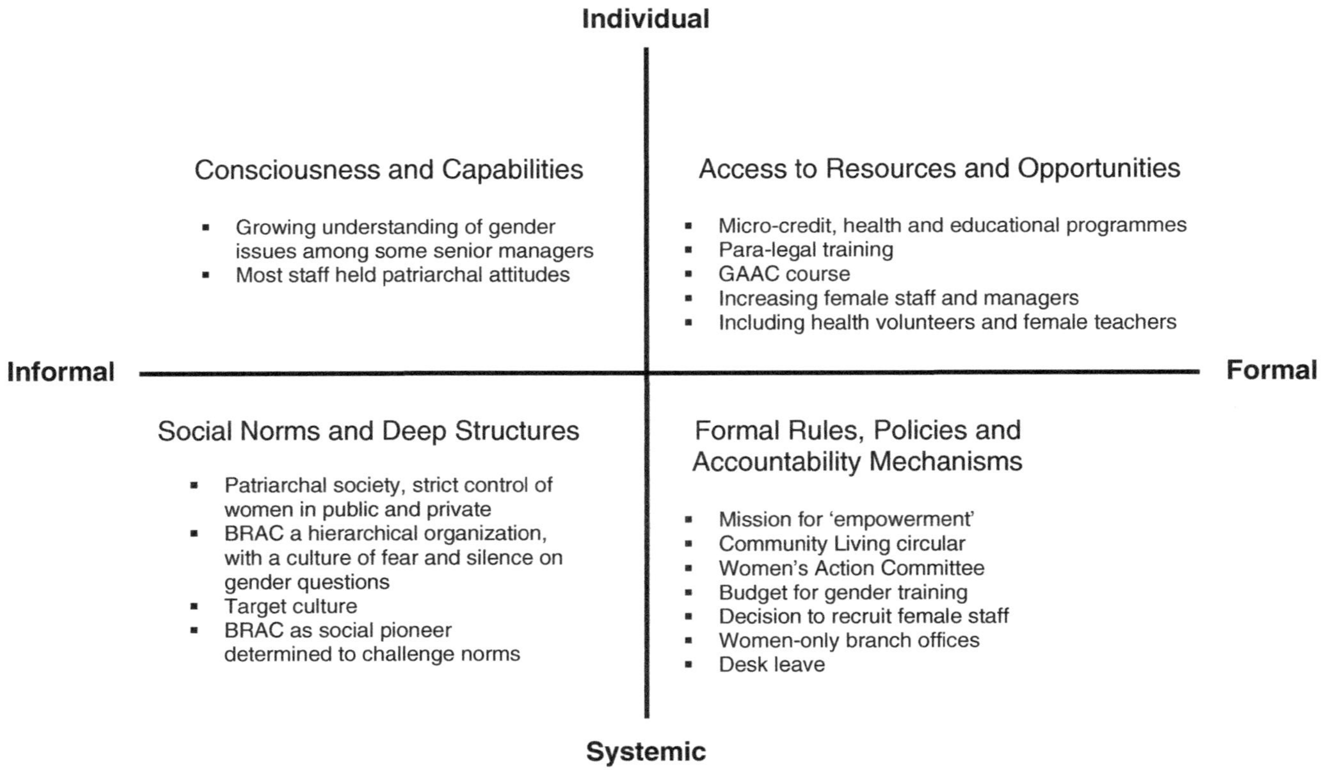

Individual

Formal

Consciousness and Capabilities

- Growing understanding of gender issues among some senior managers
- Most staff held patriarchal attitudes

Access to Resources and Opportunities

- Micro-credit, health and educational programmes
- Para-legal training
- GAAC course
- Increasing female staff and managers
- Including health volunteers and female teachers

Social Norms and Deep Structures

- Patriarchal society, strict control of women in public and private
- BRAC a hierarchical organization, with a culture of fear and silence on gender questions
- Target culture
- BRAC as social pioneer determined to challenge norms

Formal Rules, Policies and Accountability Mechanisms

- Mission for 'empowerment'
- Community Living circular
- Women's Action Committee
- Budget for gender training
- Decision to recruit female staff
- Women-only branch offices
- Desk leave

Informal

Systemic

Figure 1.3 Gender analysis of BRAC before GQAL

Notes

 1 See www.worldbank.org/en/news/press-release/2015/07/01/new-world-bank-update-shows-bangladesh-kenya-myanmar-and-tajikistan-as-middle-income-while-south-sudan-falls-back-to-low-income.
 2 See http://hdr.undp.org/sites/all/themes/hdr_theme/country-notes/BGD.pdf.
 3 See http://bbs.dhaka.gov.bd/sites/default/files/www.dhaka.gov.bd/Socio-Economic%20and%20demographic%20Report%202012.pdf; and https://mics-surveys-prod.s3.amazonaws.com/MICS5/South%20Asia/Bangladesh/2012-2013/Key%20findings/Bangladesh%202012-13%20MICS%20KFR_English.pdf.
 4 This section draws on the overview prepared for the British High Commission by Baden et al. (1994).
 5 Recent surveys have shown a decrease in domestic violence from 87 per cent in 2011 to 80 per cent in 2016. See http://bdnews24.com/bangladesh/2016/10/02/80-percent-bangladeshi-married-women-abused-by-husbands-bbs-study-finds.
 6 This section was developed based on BRAC archival documents, staff interviews and the knowledge of BRAC gender team members.
 7 Aarong was established to market handicrafts, and the cold storage facility was originally for potatoes.
 8 See www.who.int/bulletin/volumes/87/2/09-050209/en/.
 9 The findings of Goetz (1997) are based on in-depth interviews undertaken with field workers between February and October 1993, shortly before the start of discussions related to GQAL.
10 For a discussion of the evolution and management of micro-credit in BRAC see Smillie (2009).
11 The case method uses problems derived from real life to engage participants in analysis and decision-making.

References

Adnan, S. (1989) 'Birds in a Cage: Institutional Change and Women's Position in Bangladesh', *ADAB News* (Dhaka), 16: 6–7.
Baden, S., Green, C., Goetz, A.-M., Guhathakurta, M. (1994) *Background Report on Gender Issues in Bangladesh: Report Prepared for the British High Commission, Dhaka*, Brighton: Institute for Development Studies.
Blanchet, T. (1986) *Rural Women, Savings and Credit: An Anthropological View*, Dhaka: USAID.
Blanchet, T., Kramer, U. (1987) *A Plan of Action for Assistance to Women in Bangladesh*, Dhaka: Royal Norwegian Ministry of Development Co-operation.
Eggen, C. (1988) *Towards a Strategy for Women's Programming in Bangladesh: The Class and Gender Analysis; CIDA's Programme and a Work Plan*, paper prepared for country programme analyst, Ottawa: Canadian International Development Agency.
Jalal, Firoz (n.d.) *Study Report on Women in the Fifth and Seventh Parliaments of Bangladesh: A Study on Opinion of Women Members of Parliament (MPs), Governance and Democracy Team*, Dhaka: USAID/Dhaka.
Ghuznavi, F. (2008) *From Action Learning to Learning to Act: Lessons from GQAL*, Dhaka: BRAC.
Goetz, A.-M. (1997) 'Managing Organisational Change: The "Gendered" Organisation of Space and Time', *Gender and Development*, 5.1: 17–27.
Goetz, A.-M., Sen Gupta, R. (1996) 'Who Takes the Credit? Gender, Power, and Control over Loan Use in Rural Credit Programmes in Bangladesh', *World Development*, 24.1: 45–63.

Hafiza, S., (2013) 'Change is Possible: The Case of BRAC's Gender Quality Action Learning (GQAL) in Bangladesh', unpublished paper, Dhaka: BRAC.

Jahan, R. (1989) *Women and Development in Bangladesh: Challenges and Opportunities*, Dhaka: Ford Foundation.

Lukes, S. (2006) *Power: A Radical View*, 2nd edition, London: Macmillan.

Nazneen, S. (2007) 'Gender Sensitive Accountability of Service Delivery NGOs: BRAC and PROSHIKA in Bangladesh', D.Phil. dissertation, Brighton: University of Sussex.

Rao, A., Kelleher, D. (2002) *Unravelling Institutionalized Gender Inequality*, Occasional Paper #8, Toronto: Association for Women in Development.

Rao, A., Stuart, R., Kelleher, D. (1999) *Gender at Work: Organizational Change for Equality*, Hartford: Kumarian Press. Rao, A., Sandler, J., Kelleher, D., Miller, C. (2016) *Gender at Work: Theory and Practice for 21st Century Organizations*, Abingdon: Routledge.

Smillie, I., (2009) *Freedom from Want*, Sterling: Kumarian Press.

2 Strengthening BRAC's ability to advance gender equality

The team: what we were trying to do

Three international consultants and four BRAC staff from its Training Division constituted the core team that developed and led the GQAL Programme.[1] As a team, they combined expertise in gender equality, organizational development, adult education, international development and in-depth experience working in BRAC's rural development programmes and staff training.

There were three main strands of knowledge that framed our approach, rooted in theories of women's empowerment, organizational change and quality improvement and management.

Women's empowerment and gender transformation

When we began our work, 'women's empowerment' was part of the vernacular at BRAC but there was not a clear, agreed-upon understanding of what it meant. We realized that we could not just decide what it meant for BRAC; we needed to build an understanding of empowerment in consultation with staff and managers, an understanding that would make sense to them. Thus, we spent some time debating just what we, as a team, meant by the idea of women's empowerment.

Ultimately, we defined 'women's empowerment' as *the capacity of women to be economically self-sufficient and self-reliant, with control over decisions affecting their life options, and to be free from violence.* We conceptualized working toward gender transformations in terms of:

1 increasing women's and men's ability to analyse and reshape socially constructed gender relations to transform power relationships;
2 equitable access to and control over both public and private resources;
3 equitable participation in household, community and national decision-making; and
4 reshaping social institutions and organizations to include women's and men's varied perceptions and to benefit both groups.

We felt this understanding of empowerment was applicable to both BRAC's women clients and women staff. We believed these strategies could help to move the organization beyond a male–female power nexus towards gender transformation. We sought to do so by engaging women and men on issues that both united and divided them, including issues of class and privilege.

A key idea in our dialogue with BRAC was that gender does not mean 'women'. The team took the approach that we were not only concerned with women's empowerment; we were also trying to alter the relationship between men and women so that it would be characterized by greater equity and an ability, on the part of both women and men, to negotiate and agree on needs.

Compared with other thinking, this approach may seem unambitious. Acker (1992), for example, challenges us to deal with larger and more systemic issues:

> Long term strategies will have to challenge the privileging of 'economy' over life and raise questions about the rationality of such things as organisational and work commitment as well as the legitimacy of the organisation's claim for the priority of their goals over more broad goals. The gendered structure of organisations will only be completely changed with a fundamental reorganisation of both production and reproduction.
>
> (Acker, 1992: 565)

Batliwala (2007) highlights the complexity of empowerment by describing its three critical strands:

1   challenging the ideologies that justify social inequality, e.g. gender and caste;
2   changing prevailing patterns of access to and control over economic, natural and intellectual resources; and
3   transforming the institutions that reinforce and sustain power structures (such as the family, state, market, education system and media).

Kate Young's definition of empowerment involves women 'taking control over their own lives, organising to help each other, making demands on the state and on society to change ... not just ... getting power but those holding power relinquishing it' (Young, 1993: 158) quoted in Razavi and Miller, 1995: 34). In other words, for women to be empowered, the men who hold power must be receptive to and allow for its redistribution.

Goetz (1992: 15) is also clear about how extensive such change should be. As she argues, 'tinkering with structures, procedures, or representative bureaucracy' is not enough to challenge gendered power relationships and systems. She also allows that this line of thinking brings 'practical organisational change to an inaccessible level', and that we need to find ways of actively disorganizing gendered processes within organizations and between organizations and society.

These various conceptualizations were very much in our heads as we discussed the meaning of empowerment with BRAC and among ourselves, but we were also aware that, to our knowledge, no one had implemented such ideas within the context of an organizational change project. Our question was not what empowerment should mean, but rather what understanding we would use as a platform for an effective change process.

As we wrote about the process in 1999,

> Diagnosis for organisational change is a collaborative attempt to aid a system to understand itself in its own terms; it … focus[es] on the client's perception of what needs to change and how. Working with gender complicates the process, because we are not simply responding to the client's view, but we are [advancing] new concepts as well. We created new knowledge through collective conceptualisation with the staff and managers.
>
> (Rao *et al.*, 1999: 39–40)

One example of this dialogue emerged in discussion with a BRAC senior manager. As he said, 'it is difficult to win a race running on only one leg'. During an early meeting to discuss what gender equality meant, and why it was important, he proposed a race from one end of the hall to the other, in which gender discrimination against women was represented by half the staff grabbing one foot and hopping on one leg, with the other half free to run on both legs. Of course, it was no contest. This situation, he explained, was why BRAC needed to support gender equality. This explanation was not based on a human rights rationale. It was based on the understanding that both women and men needed a common goal, as well as the strength and skills to alleviate their families' poverty and insecurity. Gender equality was relevant for BRAC staff in creating a 'winning team' as well as in delivering effective programming and transforming the lives of clients, women as well as men.

Eventually, we ended up with an approach that connected with and extended the understanding of empowerment that BRAC staff and managers held. We were, in the words of Remi Rikken, a participant in the 1991 Bergen conference on gender training, 'treading sacred ground'. To navigate this difficult terrain, we looked at ways to bring people into the process, watching where the water flowed and then stepping into the current. We worked, in other words, on the basis of the context in which we found ourselves.

As a starting point, achieving a common understanding of greater gender equality as desirable – and changing behaviour to support this – was felt to be a sufficiently ambitious and achievable challenge. The team felt that institutional blockages to 'winning the race' could be tackled as they became visible through the process of change. This rationale was widely understood and supported in BRAC. Also, we believed that our approach posed no barrier to the types of constraints we could address, whether it was attitudinal change, norms change, access to resources or policy change. This belief was later challenged by Nazneen (2007). We discuss this in the Conclusion.

Organizational change

The second strand of the team's approach came from the theory and practice of organizational development and change. The change strategy we developed was grounded in the practices and assumptions of collaborative change described by such writers as Senge (1990) and Weisbord (1987). The thinking in this area had paid no attention to gender, although Goetz's article on gender and public administration (Goetz, 1992) had highlighted the organizational dynamics that block gender equality. Later work (Hearn, 2000; Rao *et al.*, 1999; Connell, 2002; Krook and Mackay, 2011) brought together thinking about organizations, change and gendered institutions. But when we began with BRAC, this thread of our thinking was heavily influenced by contemporary ideas of organizational learning and development.

Our understanding of organizational change emphasized the importance of seeing the organization (and its surrounding context) as an organic system of relationships of influence. Individuals (even powerful ones) did not act alone. They functioned within a context of relationships and norms, which both constrain them and make certain actions possible. It was this system of norms and relationships we wanted to influence.

Organizational development was an approach to change that combined management sponsorship and support with bottom-up participation to define the nature of the change. In many ways, this bottom-up approach challenged BRAC's hierarchical culture, but we believed that challenging hierarchy was part of what we needed to do. Some senior managers were quite supportive of this challenge. For example, the head of the Training Division wanted to break the 'blame and avoid responsibility' model that he felt characterized BRAC.

Bennis, Benne and Chin (1968) named this family of strategies 'normative/ re-educative', in contrast with 'coercive' strategies that attempt to pressure or shame managers into change or 'rational' strategies that attempt to convince them through logical reasoning. We adopted normative/re-educative strategies in large part because more top-down measures have a high failure rate: between 60 and 70 per cent fail (Heffernan, 2015; Kotter, 1995). A normative, re-educative approach works with the heart and the head by supporting a learning process that anticipates and accepts psychological resistance to the change of fundamental attitudes. This strategy for organizational change has the following features:

- The change process is rooted in systemic elements, such as norms, structures and organizational policies.
- The organization must 'own' the change goals. The change agents cannot impose the goals. The role of the change agent is to help the organization achieve the goals it has chosen.
- The process is long term (two to five years).
- It is both systemic and personal. It focuses on systemic changes and on the individual learning of organizational members.
- It is data-based. It is not informed by universal prescriptions but by the specific requirements of that organization as demonstrated by a collaborative data-collection and analysis process.
- The change agent is not expected to enter as an expert and prescribe the nature of the change. Her/his primary role is facilitator or catalyst,

although from time to time she/he must be prepared to give advice, particularly in the process, timing and staging of the change.

This organizational change approach was well aligned with and informed by the adult education theories of Paulo Freire (2000) and Robert Kegan (Kegan and Lahey, 2009) that the team espoused and practised, and that were also familiar to BRAC. Freire worked with poor indigenous communities in Brazil to examine the beliefs, structures and processes that oppressed them collectively, to raise their consciousness to believe and act in their own interests. He hypothesized that oppressed people internalized the dominant beliefs of their culture about their own low status, and that a process of collective reflection and analysis could help them reject their sense of inferiority and organize for change. Kegan, based at Harvard, helped people to examine why they behave in self-destructive or self-limiting ways, and to take a series of incremental steps to shift their behaviour.

Both Freire and Kegan used people's real-life experiences and feelings, not theoretical knowledge, to ground their pedagogy. Like them, we aimed not to tell people what to think, but to help them understand how and why they think and act the way they do, so they can make choices about how they live their lives as individuals and as communities.

The understandings described above could lead to a variety of interventions. The approach we chose – 'action-learning' (Kelleher, 2009) – is a *process that supports teams of people who work together to use their differing perspectives to learn how to do something that runs counter to their normal work habits*. It gives staff a chance fully to understand the implications of an action that management wants to undertake, and gives them an active role in making it happen. It is different from 'learning by doing' in that it is not rote practice of a new skill, but requires intellectual effort and judgement to identify the skill that is needed, practice to develop expertise, and dialogue with colleagues to review whether the intentions are in fact being met or whether more learning is required.

Quality Improvement or Total Quality Management

The third element of our approach was rooted in Quality Improvement or Total Quality Management (TQM), which grew out of the need, in the private sector, to respond to intense competition by constantly improving production systems to provide customers with what they want, when they want it. It was pioneered by 'quality circles' in Japanese automakers, described by Edward Demmings and popularized by Pascale and Athos (1981). [2] Companies found that they needed to focus not on profits, but on the customer. It eventually meant restructuring the relationship between workers and management.

The integration of this element came from a concern, on the part of BRAC's Executive Director, that staff should be better able to take initiative to understand and solve problems, rather than obey orders. This approach, he felt, would be needed as BRAC grew. Investing in command and control processes for a larger organization dealing with ever more complex issues would have diminishing returns. The existing culture of obeying orders, which reflected BRAC's strict programmatic standards and targets and the intentional design of tasks so they could be completed by people with limited formal education, had the disadvantage, per the Director of Training, of discouraging staff to take initiative in problem-solving. Instead, it generated a culture of 'shifting responsibility' in which a staff member's default position when faced with problems was to suggest those problems fell outside her/his area of responsibility, and were instead caused by the negligence or miscommunications of people either higher or lower in the hierarchy. It was up to the person giving the orders to foresee and prevent problems. So, for example, if the truck delivering day-old chicks arrived after dark, it was not the Programme Officer's responsibility to ensure they were delivered or kept warm overnight for women to collect the next day. Instead, it was the truck driver's responsibility to be on time.

For an organization such as BRAC, quality first and foremost relates to programme outcomes and impact. BRAC's very existence is premised on its ability to support poor women and men in their individual and collective efforts to improve their situation. In the final analysis, BRAC's worth is measured in these terms. In BRAC, TQM could provide a balance to the focus on quantitative targets and measurements. It would focus on constant improvement of the quality of service to members and continue to push the boundaries of empowerment beyond delivery of services to strengthening women's self-reliance. It would involve staff and members in programme design and monitoring, exploring avenues of strengthening the collective organizations of members and their participation in community decision-making bodies, and the role of men and women in this process. It would ask staff who deliver services to be part of an ongoing structured analysis of how those services could be more effective and delivered at lower cost.

In bringing these three elements of the approach together, therefore, the team chose to define 'gender issues' in terms that made sense to BRAC: *anything that hindered, prevented or restricted women's (either staff or programme beneficiaries) involvement in the delivery, analysis and improvement of a programme.* Because this definition is quite broad, it allowed a spectrum of intervention targets. Some of the things that prevented women staff's full participation in quality programme delivery and improvement were cultural; some were attitudinal; and some were organizational. For example, attitudinally and culturally, women's effective participation meant that they needed the opportunity to earn the respect of their male colleagues; that men in BRAC needed to be able to understand the situation faced by both village women and women staff in BRAC. Organizationally, arrangements such as allocating leave and accommodating overnight guests at the Area Office needed to be improved so that women could better integrate their work and their family lives. Deficiencies in such arrangements affected both women and men, but women were more affected because it was less acceptable for them to travel.

Administering diagnostic tools to establish a baseline

In the spring of 1994, the team conducted a series of consultations and 23 needs-assessment workshops with 400 staff (approximately 20 per cent of whom were women) at all levels, from part-time teachers and health workers to senior managers, across BRAC's three main programmes: Rural Development, Non-formal Primary Education, and Health and Family Planning. We also conducted a survey of 258 BRAC staff, 40 per cent of whom were women. This survey, which consisted of 22 questions, was designed to gauge staff attitudes and values regarding BRAC's organizational processes and the gendered dimensions of its programmes. Survey data complemented the data gathered in the two-day needs-assessment workshops, each of which explored empowerment issues related to programmes and gender issues related to organizational life.

The team also selected four Area Offices (in the districts of Mymensingh, Rajshahi and Pabna) on the basis of criteria related to geographic and economic diversity and programme performance to provide valid and compelling data for gender-related strategic planning as well as an orientation to gender thinking to a cross-section of BRAC staff and to deepen the research team's own understanding of gender issues relevant to BRAC. Informing this exercise were the team's ongoing efforts to deconstruct theoretical formulations of power, women's empowerment and gender equality.

Empowerment: conceptual clarity for field-level application

The first two exercises in the workshops aimed at assessing:

- the quality of BRAC staff's conceptual understanding of women's empowerment issues;
- how and to what extent staff applied these concepts to field-level situations;
- staff's ideas on how BRAC should change or improve its programmes to further the empowerment of women; and
- what kinds of support staff would need to implement these changes.

To assess staff's understanding of women's empowerment, the team asked participants to articulate key differences between poor women and men in rural Bangladesh along the three major dimensions of empowerment: access to and control over income and resources; knowledge of and the ability to negotiate for one's rights; and control over one's own body and security of movement. Then participants were asked to probe the reasons for these differences and suggest what should be done to make the situation more gender equitable.

To understand how staff worked on the ground on women's empower-ment, they were asked to analyse the key empowerment dimensions through brief case studies that posed real-life problems encountered by BRAC in its programmes. The case studies asked participants to develop actions in response to particular issues. The Gender Team developed a total of six cases for use in this exercise. The first three cases focused on the three empower-ment dimensions mentioned above; the last three focused on health, educa-tion and income-generating skills. We have included one of the cases ('The story of Rohim') as an example.[3]

Inside BRAC: conditions and relationships

To assess internal organizational issues, three exercises were developed. The first encouraged participants to write, individually and anonymously, about positive as well as problematic aspects of working in BRAC. The 'problems' and 'successes' were collected and later distributed to the group, which categorized them by type: living conditions; working conditions; career development; and relationships with supervisors, colleagues and VO members. Groups chose the most important testimonies and discussed what could be done to deal with the problems they raised. In the second exercise, participants were given two cases for discussion, both of which focused on intra-organizational gender dynamics. One case illustrated women's lack of voice; the other, norms of purity and appropriate behaviour for women.

The story of Rohim

Rohim was cycling back from the village women borrowers (VO) meeting where he had collected loan payments, but his mind was not on the traffic, the rice greening in the paddy fields or the villagers' greetings. He was thinking about his conversation with Sakina, one of the BRAC members. She had given her loan repayment, but she seemed sad. He knew Sakina quite well, so he had asked her privately if she was all right. She had told him that the repayment money had come from the village moneylender, because her husband had taken the money from the paddy husking and invested it in buying pulses for future sale. When she protested, he said that he was responsible for making decisions in the family and beat her to make her behave. This sad story worried Rohim. He knew that this happened to some of the other women in his groups, while others were able to make decisions about money with their husbands harmoniously. Some cases were even worse than Sakina's, with husbands spending the proceeds from their wives' labour in the teashops. Rohim himself was so busy just collecting the money and accounting for it that he felt unable even to think about what to do. Was this situation his responsibility? It was not easy to think of what he or BRAC could do to help Sakina and those like her. Maybe he should just shrug his shoulders and forget about it.

Discussion questions

1   What is the problem or problems in this case?
2   If you were the BRAC staff member in this case, what would you do to deal with this problem(s)?
3   What should BRAC do to deal with this problem(s)?
4   What support or training would you need to deal with this problem(s)?

The third exercise involved participants describing, pictorially and verbally, their preferred vision of BRAC's organizational future, based on their conceptions of appropriate gender roles and appropriate organizational responses in support of gender equality. One example was based on the 'Fable of the fox and the crane', which is now common in gender-awareness sessions but was quite novel at the time.[4] Using visuals, the participants are introduced to the fable, which goes something like this:

> The fox invited the crane to dinner. He served the food on a large flat dish. The crane, with her long, narrow beak could not eat. The crane invited the fox to dinner. She served the food in a deep vase, so the fox with his short, wide face could not eat.

Participants are asked:

• How does the crane feel when invited to the fox's house for dinner?
• How does the fox feel when invited to the crane's house?
• Are they able to benefit equally from the food?
• Is this fair?
• Why or why not?

The point being introduced is that, while both friends had an equal opportunity for nourishment, each time they met, one of them could not take advantage of this opportunity. The story helps to reinforce the idea that equal treatment does not always mean the same treatment, and that it is important to identify barriers to accessing opportunities. The exercise also encourages participants to consider different scenarios to ensure that both the fox and the crane can access food equally (i.e., access equality of outcomes), for example by ensuring that they are each served food in a dish that is appropriate to their physiology or designing a dish that they could *both* use. Participants were asked to apply the fable to BRAC as an organization in terms of the treatment of women and men staff, and to think about the kind of adjustments BRAC could make that they thought were appropriate.

Findings of the needs–assessment exercise

The findings of the needs–assessment exercise fell into three broad areas: staff attitudes about women's empowerment and female staff; gender analysis and programming; and gender and organizational issues.

Staff attitudes

The assessment showed that staff, both male and female, at all levels and across all programmes, believed BRAC should pursue women's empowerment and change men's and women's attitudes and values as a prerequisite to accomplishing this goal. Beyond this, however, there were uncertainties and disagreements about programming strategies, particularly in the areas of women's mobility, intra-household decision-making and conflict, and ensuring freedom from violence.

Most staff also believed that women should be promoted up the management ladder. But there was a good deal of disagreement over questions of reconciling women's family and work responsibilities, granting special provisions to women staff, and building an accelerated career path for women. Gender relations in the workplace were often not smooth and women faced varying levels of teasing and/or harassment. Thus, while conditions had improved for women in the years before 1994, a great deal remained to be done.

Understanding gender issues

Three issues stood out regarding BRAC staff's conceptual understanding of gender issues and their application of this understanding to programmatic situations. First, staff's intuitive understanding of gender differences did not often translate into proposing creative and strategic solutions for dealing with the core issues. Instead, proposals tended either to sacrifice empowerment goals in the name of programmatic efficiency (reaching targets) or respond in standard ways to symptoms of gender inequality rather than present solutions to address inequality at its roots. Staff repeatedly cited the negative fallout from over-ambitious targets set without consideration for regional variations. Combined with the imperative of expanded area coverage and membership, this translated into a numbers race and resulted in less and less time for the pursuit of pro-grammatic excellence and assessment of qualitative impact. Already the strains of this strategy were apparent. Supervisors did not want to hear about imple-mentation problems, and staff, fearful of their supervisors' wrath, kept problems hidden. As discussed in Chapter 1, performance was measured against achieve-ment of rigid targets and staff were punished for failure. For example, if weekly credit repayments were not met, staff were blamed for their inefficiency and forced to make up the total amount due from their own salaries.

Second, staff searched for harmonious solutions to problems of women's subordination in the family and community, rather than proposed interventions that could invite conflict and confrontation. In the Bangladeshi cultural and political context, this was instructive and strategic, but also worrisome, because it could leave the power imbalance and gender ideology intact. However, defining what is empowering in each context can be difficult. For example, Naila Kabeer (1998) distinguishes between 'objective' criteria of empowerment imposed from the outside, which treat women as atomized individuals and link their empowerment with individualized behaviour, and empowerment defined from the point of view of women themselves, who live within structural and social constraints.

This understanding led us to be tentatively open to the possibility that change in power relations was not always based on obvious zero-sum assumptions; rather, in some conditions everyone's power and well-being could increase under more egalitarian conditions. This idea was very attractive to staff. It led us to push participants to question in what situations win–win solutions were feasible.

The needs assessment posed this problematic of zero-sum assumptions about power through contrasting stories about everyday situations faced by women and men in Bangladeshi society. For example, there was a story about two brothers who fought about the division between them of inherited land, while two other brothers in the same situation decided to farm together. There was another story where a young woman saved her family by transgressing the rules that prevented her from leaving her homestead. Participants found these stories compelling, grappled with the underlying assumptions, and were able to develop criteria for analysing and creatively reframing power dynamics in different situations. They concluded that while some power relations are indeed zero-sum, many are not, or could be transformed. The assessment team used images to convey the difference between finite goods, like a cake, which is gone once it is eaten, and social goods, like a candle, which can light many others without being used up itself.

Third, BRAC staff placed inordinate emphasis on and had enormous faith in the ability to change behaviours and values through training. To this extent, they discounted (and therefore inadequately addressed) the tremendous impact of forces external to the individual (family, kinship, factions, cultural norms, gender ideology, etc.) in shaping individual behaviour.

Put together, staff responses painted a complex picture. BRAC was an organization in transition from a collective to a corporation, committed to pursuing empowerment goals in a volatile socio-economic and political environment. Publicly, it was grappling with an enormous expansion in area coverage and an increasing complexity and technical sophistication in programme content. There was a growing backlash from religious fundamentalists about the work of NGOs, which had reached a high point in 1993, when groups rioted and burned school buildings.

Internally, the complexity that is routinely found in a large organization was exacerbated by several features:

- a race to meet targets that left experienced supervisors with little time to nurture and guide newer staff;

- newcomers fresh out of university who were moving up the organizational ladder quickly and being handed programme responsibility;
- a management style focused on target achievement that discouraged searches for lasting solutions to difficult problems of women's subordination and gender-equitable change;
- an organisational environment in which opportunities for open discussion on personal and professional issues were becoming scarce;
- a brewing conflict between those who upheld traditional patriarchal norms and behaviours and others who embraced the nascent culture of encouraging gender equality (a culture supported at the very highest levels of policy-making);
- a need to forge ways of working between men and women in an organization that espoused countercultural values but among people who did not necessarily believe in them;
- fatigue among longstanding cadres in the front-line fight for gender equality; and
- a desire for work–family balance among men and women staff alike.

Developing and negotiating an action–learning plan

In July 1994, the team held a strategic planning meeting with all senior BRAC managers over two and a half days to analyse the needs-assessment data systematically, develop a vision of what BRAC wanted to accomplish in terms of women's empowerment, and agree on a strategy for accomplishing that mission. The team consolidated the findings of the baseline as follows:

- BRAC staff were ambivalent and not deeply knowledgeable about women's empowerment, but there was a strong belief among staff that BRAC should improve its efforts to empower poor rural women.
- There was a culture of silence and obedience, which was rooted in the arbitrary nature of supervisory relations. This culture made organizational learning difficult.
- BRAC had a strong tradition of and considerable competence in training.
- BRAC was focused on quantity of outputs, for example percentage of loans repaid and number of schools opened. This was a great strength and BRAC exceeded the capacity of many NGOs in this regard, but there was an insufficient focus on programmatic quality and whether programmes changed the quality of women's lives.
- BRAC had a tradition of organizational evaluation and a significant research establishment.
- BRAC was facing challenges from fundamentalist and other groups in Bangladesh whose interests were threatened by BRAC's success.
- Living and working conditions were difficult for women in BRAC. There was a difference of opinion as to whether women should have different working conditions or should 'tough it out', like the men did.

- BRAC's rapid growth provided both opportunities and constraints for changes in gender relations.

The team also proposed two working hypotheses:

1   Simply teaching large numbers of BRAC staff about gender relations would not change the way BRAC worked with its members or how women were treated in the organization. What was needed was change at a more basic level in how the organization functioned, in its very culture.
2   Many methods of organizational intervention spring from Western culture and would need to be adapted in ways that made sense in the South Asian context and to BRAC.

When we presented the results of the needs assessment many objected strongly to the 'culture of silence' analysis. In retrospect, the reaction of many of BRAC's senior managers is understandable. If there was a culture of silence, we should have realized people might be reluctant to talk about it. Managers did not come to a decision during the July workshop, and visioning and strategizing work continued as BRAC underwent its own internal strategic planning exercise for the fourth phase of its Rural Development Programme in August.

We took the managers' objections seriously and reviewed our data. We confirmed our analysis and began a process of meeting with the Executive Director and many of the senior managers in one-to-one meetings. In these meetings, we also discussed the emerging ideas we were developing regarding a programme that could address these issues.

Ultimately, after several months of discussion and negotiation, the team suggested building on BRAC's strengths in training, research and innovation by organizing groups of staff to undertake 'action learning', which in this case meant identifying and analysing selected gender-related problems and potential solutions and negotiating their testing and revision with the intent of replicating successes across programmes. During action-learning processes, staff considered proposals such as increasing women beneficiaries' control of their own earnings, retaining and promoting a higher percentage of women staff, and addressing gender issues in the Area Offices where women and men lived and worked together. The GQAL Team would go on to train facilitators to support the action learning.

A key turning point in these negotiations was the moment when we realized that, while we were advocates for gender equality, we were also consultants to BRAC and needed to see the world through their eyes. We met with the Director of the RDP and asked how we could do this in a way that helped him achieve his goals. This was the meeting in which we were able to find common ground. It emerged that his preference was to hold shorter GQAL sessions in Area Offices rather than longer sessions in local training centres. Doing so would present less of a time burden for Area Office staff.

One key advantage of the action-learning approach, the team felt, was that a large number of staff and middle managers would be learning gender-related organizational problem-solving techniques and would be responsible for designing solutions. Another advantage was that it could invite open discussion and creative thinking and allow senior and middle managers to talk about this aspect of BRAC's organizational and programmatic life. Finally, our model of action learning was seen as sufficiently close to previous residential training at BRAC, such that it fitted into a broader training structure. The Gender Team took advantage of BRAC's competence in, and valuing of, staff training.

In the fall, BRAC decided that a pilot phase of GQAL should be conducted in Area Offices, overseen by Regional Directors at their periodic meetings. The team proceeded to develop and implement the agreed-on action-learning programme, which was called Gender Quality Action Learning (GQAL). Middle and senior managers did not undertake their own action learning focused on issues relevant to their level. Instead, they supervised what was happening in the action learning at Area Offices and met regularly with the GQAL team to review progress and challenges.

How is action learning different from training?

Although action learning had enough similarities to gender training that BRAC could imagine proceeding with it with Training Division staff, there are some fundamental differences between the two approaches. We have already mentioned that the learning would happen in teams comprising people who worked together, and that the process was meant to be continuous over one year. More fundamentally, action learning carries different assumptions about pedagogy and the nature of knowledge than most other gender-training programmes. In most cases, while gender training might be more or less experiential, it is about transmitting a set of understandings from trainer to participant. Rowland's description of leadership training as 'set curricula delivered through classroom-taught, rationally based, individual-focused methods' in which 'participants are taken out of their day-to-day workplaces to be inspired by expert faculty, work on case studies … and take away [the] latest thinking', could apply equally to much gender training (Rowland, 2016: 1).

In contrast, although the first few sessions of GQAL taught basic ideas about gender equality, this action learning did not have a set curriculum. It was, instead, an effort to support learners to come to new understandings that could not have been predicted before the process began. This is because learners are encouraged to diagnose their situations and craft action plans that will work in that specific cultural and organizational setting.

Regarding the nature of knowledge in action learning, two things are important. First, standard training is generally conducted away from the work environment, with participants from different parts of the organization. This means that it is conducted in a context that is free of the power dynamics that emerge in a specific work environment. 'Knowledge' is thus decontextualized.

Action learning happens within the work environment and must come to terms with the power relationships within that office. Therefore, what counts as 'knowledge' is much more specific and culturally contingent. Second, the act of 'teaching' particular ideas of gender equality to participants seems to challenge the emancipatory roots of feminism. In contrast, action learning sees learning as primarily fashioned by the participant, based on their inclination and level of understanding.

Finally, the conception of what is learned differs fundamentally in the two approaches. In most gender-training programmes, sponsors would be happy if participants increased their knowledge about gender relations and perhaps experienced some attitudinal change. Action learning is premised on an existentialist understanding that learning and life choices require *action* before they can be seen as valid.

The next chapter describes the GQAL Programme's impact on BRAC, including data collected 20 years after it was launched in 1994.

Notes

1 The original team consisted of: Aruna Rao, the external team leader, based in Dhaka, who led the GQAL process; Rieky Stuart and David Kelleher, from Canada, who provided expert input at key points in the process; Sheepa Hafiza, the BRAC team leader; and Naheed Sultana, Habibur Rahman and Sadequr Rahman from BRAC's Training Division.
2 The team felt that GQAL should include the following key Demmings principles: (1) establish clear purpose so that staff can begin a never-ending process of continual improvement; (2) drive out fear so that everyone can work effectively; (3) reinforce leadership; and (4) promote an understanding that the transformation is everybody's job.
3 These baseline assessment tools can be found in Stuart *et al.* (1997).
4 For a more recent version of this, see USAID (2012: 3).

References

Acker, J. (1992) 'From Sex Rules to Gendered Institutions', *Contemporary Sociology*, 21.5: 565–569.
Batliwala, S. (2007) 'Putting the Power Back into Empowerment', *Open Democracy*, www.opendemocracy.net/article/putting_power_back_into_empowerment_0 (accessed 2 November 2016).
Bennis, W., Benne, K., Chin, R. (1968) *The Planning of Change*, 2nd edn, New York: Holt Rinehart and Winston.
Stuart, R., Rao, A., Kelleher, D., Hafiza, S., Sultana, N., Rahman, H., Rahman, S. (1997) *BRAC Technical Manual: An Action-Learning Approach to Gender and Organisational Change*, www.brac.net/sites/default/files/BRAC-Technical-Manual-Chapter_01-07.pdf (accessed 22 February 2017).
Connell, R.W. (2002) *Gender*, Cambridge: Polity Press.
Freire, P., (2000) *Pedagogy of the Oppressed*, 30th anniversary edn, New York: Bloomsbury.
Goetz, A.-M. (1992) 'Gender and Administration', *IDS Bulletin*, 23.4: 6–17.
Goetz, A.-M., Sen Gupta, R. (1996) 'Who Takes the Credit? Gender, Power, and Control over Loan Use in Rural Credit Programmes in Bangladesh', *World Development*, 24.1: 45–63.

Hearn, J. (2000) 'On the Complexity of Feminist Interventions in Organisations', *Organisation*, 7.4: 609–624.

Kabeer, N. (1998) 'Money Can't Buy Me Love: Re-evaluating Gender Credit and Empowerment in Rural Bangladesh', IDS Discussion Paper, Brighton: Institute for Development Studies.

Kegan, R., Lahey, L. (2009) *Immunity to Change: How to Overcome It and Unlock the Potential in Yourself and Your Organization*, Cambridge, MA: Harvard University Press.

Kelleher, D. (2009) 'Action Learning for Gender Equality', http://genderatwork.org/Portals/0/Uploads/Documents/Resources/Action-Learning-for-Gender-Equality-FINAL-3_0.pdf (accessed 30 October 2016).

Kotter, J. (1995) 'Leading Change: Why Transformational Efforts Fail', *Harvard Business Review*, May–June: 92–107.

Krook, M.L., Mackay, F. (eds) (2011) *Gender, Politics and Institutions: Towards a Feminist Institutionalism*, Basingstoke: Palgrave Macmillan.

Heffernan, M. (2015) *Beyond Measure*, New York: TED Books.

Nazneen, S. (2007) 'Gender Sensitive Accountability of Service Delivery NGOs: BRAC and PROSHIKA in Bangladesh', D.Phil. dissertation, Brighton: University of Sussex.

Pascale, R., Athos, A. (1981) *The Art of Japanese Management*, New York: Simon and Schuster.

Rao, A., Kelleher, D. (2002) *Unravelling Institutionalized Gender Inequality*, Occasional Paper #8, Toronto: Association for Women in Development.

Rao, A., Sandler, J., Kelleher, D., Miller, C. (2016) *Gender at Work: Theory and Practice for 21st Century Organizations*, Abingdon: Routledge.

Rao, A., Stuart, R., Kelleher, D. (1999) *Gender at Work: Organizational Change for Equality*, Hartford: Kumarian Press.

Razavi, S., Miller, C. (1995) *From WID to GAD: Conceptual Shifts in the Women and Development Discourse*, Occasional Paper #1, Geneva: United Nations Research Institute for Social Development.

Rowland, D. (2016) 'Why Leadership Development Isn't Developing Leaders', *Harvard Business Review*, 14 October, https://hbr.org/2016/10/why-leadership-development-isnt-developing-leaders (accessed 30 October 2016).

Senge, P. (1990) *The Fifth Discipline: The Art and Science of the Learning Organization*, New York: Doubleday.

USAID (2012) *Gender Mainstreaming: Participant's Resource Book*, http://pdf.usaid.gov/pdf_docs/PA00JRZM.pdf (accessed 22 February 2017).

Weisbord, M. (1987) *Productive Workplaces*, San Francisco: Jossey-Bass.

Young, Kate (1993) *Planning Development with Women: Making a World of Difference*, New York: St Martin's Press.

3 Implementing GQAL in BRAC

Designing and testing GQAL in BRAC

As described in Chapter 2, BRAC eventually agreed that it would use an action-learning approach to help staff improve their capacity to work on gender-equality issues, both organizationally and programmatically. As proposed by Aminul Alam, Director of the RDP, GQAL began as a pilot starting at the Area Office level, with support from and monitoring by GQAL facilitators. The facilitators would be seconded from the Training Division and would meet monthly to review progress. They would report to regional management meetings within each region, and to the group of regional managers. The GQAL leadership would report to senior managers as required at headquarters.

Earlier, the GQAL Team had established principles of transparency, ownership (meaning managers owned the process and decisions could not be made without them) and holism (we were interested in both programmatic and personnel issues, attitudes and perceptions).

The GQAL Team continued to follow the principle of 'ownership' of the process among BRAC managers and departments, and developed two more principles that guided its work: 'no surprises', making sure that issues would be dealt with transparently and proactively as they arose, modelling the problem-solving approach we wanted to instil in BRAC; and 'political knitting', actively communicating and linking between levels and units that normally worked on their own, in order to address issues that affected BRAC both vertically and horizontally.

Initially, BRAC managers wanted to reach 1,500 people via the pilot pro-gramme. Constraints in the availability of facilitators for such a large-scale pilot, as well as in the capacity of the Gender Team to manage such a large number of diverse interventions, led to the pilot covering only 900 field-level staff in 28 RDP Area Offices in Rajshahi, Pabna, Nawgaon and Sirajganj and 8 HPD offices in Mymensingh.

The team decided that each office should spend three initial sessions of three hours each for their introduction to the action-learning process. The first session would introduce the process. The second would engage participants in pre-liminary learning about inequalities in gender relations, and would introduce the concept of biological and socially constructed differences between women and men, as well as the sexual division of labour. The third would help participants reflect on how change takes place at both a personal and an organizational level. The goal of these three sessions was to introduce the 'triangle' of programme quality, gender equality and change.

In the fourth session office staff would select an issue to work on, based on their own priorities and three criteria: the degree to which the issue related to gender inequality; the degree to which the issue would contribute to and be important to BRAC; and the capacity of the office staff to learn about and act on the chosen issue.[1] They would analyse the issue, choose one or more related causes to learn about and act on, and then develop and implement a learning/action plan. One of the more helpful tools was the 'Web Chart' shown in Figure 3.1. Completing a web diagram allowed participants to analyse the causes of a particular issue, then the causes of the causes, and, finally, to choose some 'actionable' cause they could build a plan to work on.

The final step would be an evaluation of the entire process and its results by the office staff teams as well as the Gender Team.

The facilitators would meet with each office each month to lead the initial orientation sessions and then facilitate the steps of the action-learning process.

The GQAL cycle is illustrated in Figure 3.2.

Facilitators would also meet monthly with the Gender Team and with the relevant BRAC managers to share feedback, build skills, plan the next round of sessions, solve problems, ensure quality control, express solidarity, co-ordinate the programme and monitor progress. The BRAC staff on the Gender Team would supervise and support the facilitators.

Training of trainers

Four members of the Gender Team (David Kelleher, Rieky Stuart, Sheepa Hafiza and Sadequr Rahman) met for five days to plan the Training of Trainers (TOT) session. BRAC had agreed that the team would work with all the staff in the selected Area Office. As discussed in Chapter 2, working with 'intact teams' – people who normally work together – would increase the possibility of action to reinforce learning and change. Of course, this limited the time available for the action-learning sessions, since it was not easy to shut down an entire office for a long period of time.

In planning the TOT session, the Gender Team decided to adopt a very simple process. They prepared the lesson plans for the first three orientation sessions. They began the TOT with some group building, then modelled each lesson, divided the facilitators into three small groups and worked with each group as they prepared to lead a session. Participants drew lots before the presentation to determine which facilitator would present the session to their peers in the small group.

Each presentation was videotaped. After each trial, the presenters would assess their own facilitation, the audience of peers would give feedback, and the

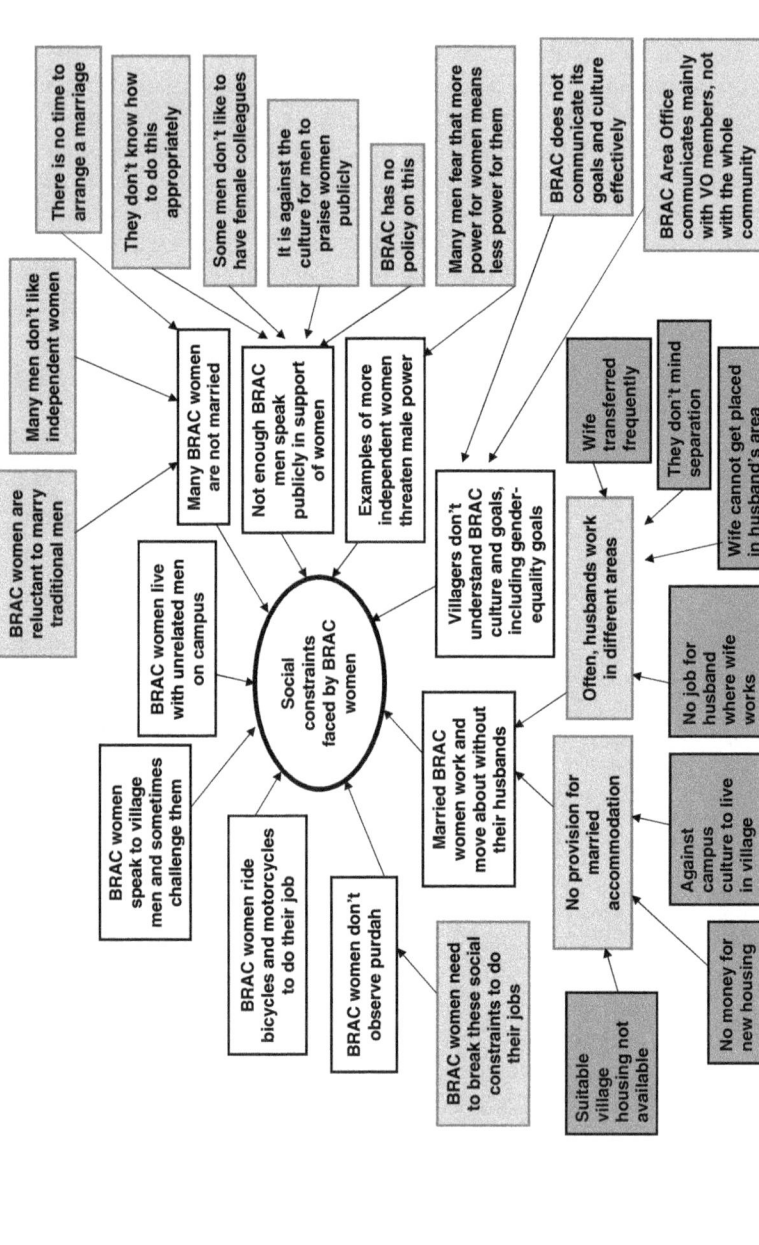

Figure 3.1 Social constraints faced by BRAC women

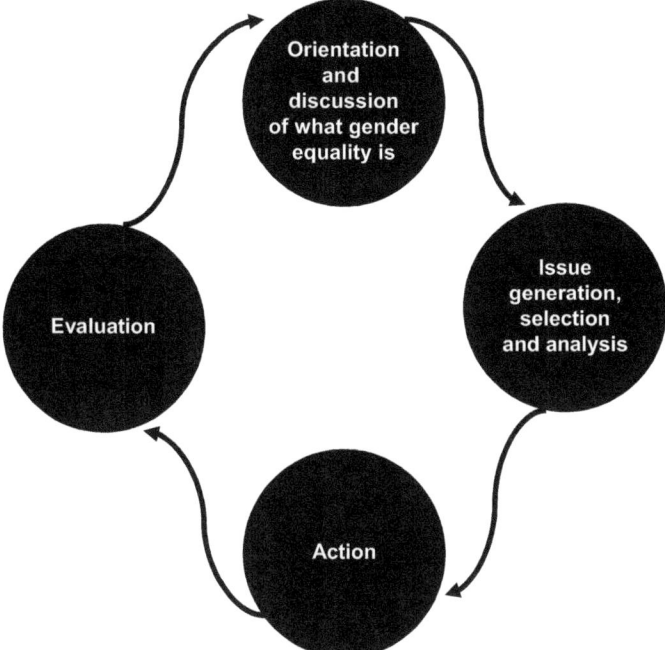

Figure 3.2 The GQAL cycle

lead trainers (the Gender Team members) would also give feedback. Participants were given time for preparation and free time in the evenings to review
the videos (this turned out to be a popular pastime). Each morning, a small
group of participants was invited to summarize key elements of the previous
day and present a mini-lecture or training addressing an issue that had arisen
during the previous day. We called this a 'miniversity'.

This process proved very fruitful. The trainers and participants were able to
find a number of problems in the original lesson plans, make corrections and
remodel the sessions. All participants found this openness both stimulating and
demanding. At each stage, the facilitators learned by living the process in which
making mistakes was an effective source of learning and improvement.

Participants also discovered how an open-ended learning or problem-solving
process is different from training that delivers predetermined conclusions; how
it 'feels' different to participants and facilitators and requires different skills and
attitudes. For example, the deconstruction of assumptions about whether
changes in power relations are zero-sum (described in the needs-assessment
findings in Chapter 2) is an excellent example of open-ended learning that
encourages reflection and participation. Techniques for open-ended learning –
such as posing open questions rather than closed ones, using contrast or paradox,
telling stories and using participatory methods – were presented and demonstrated. This approach to adult education, modelled on Freire's principles, was

at first regarded with some scepticism by BRAC trainers, but it became one of the hallmarks of GQAL and continues to be used by Gender at Work, the NGO that grew out of the BRAC work and similar experiences.

Every participant had a chance to lead at least part of one session. Those who had two chances improved their performance markedly on the second occasion (about two-thirds of the TOT participants were chosen to become GQAL facilitators). One of the challenges in designing these sessions was to keep them within the skill and experience range of the facilitators. Most were experienced trainers, but they were used to a top-down delivery of courses. Their exposure to gender and development issues was usually limited to their participation in BRAC's five-day Gender Awareness and Analysis course. The leadership team felt that the monthly sessions with the Gender Team were essential to build skills as the action-learning process got under way, to monitor progress and to continue improving the process and the facilitators' skills. The team also felt that it would need to continue to support the development of a new role for the facilitators: as it worked with office staff 'teams', it risked being caught between senior managers and field staff if tensions or problems developed. For example, early in the process, some of the Area Managers complained that the facilitators were siding with the participants in finding fault with the managers. An important role of the monthly GQAL meetings was to model and reinforce constructive relationships among *all* the players and find solutions to these tensions. The meetings were also important for the trainers to connect with the programme leadership and update those leaders on progress in the field.

Although some of the Gender Team felt that the Training Division had not sent their best trainers to GQAL, it soon became known that 'GQAL has the best trainers'.[2]

Rohim's story illustrates how one GQAL facilitator experienced the programme.

It isn't easy but it's important: Rohim's story[3]

Rohim was tired. He had travelled all day to get to Rajshahi, then spent a difficult evening with the Area Manager (AM). He was supposed to start a GQAL action-learning programme the next day, but his arrival was not encouraging: the AM told him to return to Dhaka because his staff had no time for training. 'We have repayments to collect,' the AM said. 'My staff has to work. Training isn't work.'

Rohim had patiently explained that GQAL was happening all over Bangladesh and that it actually improved the staff's effectiveness in meeting the needs of women clients. The AM wasn't buying it, but Rohim showed him the letter from Fazle Abed, the Executive Director of BRAC, telling AMs that this programme was very important and that he expected their co-operation. Ultimately, the AM relented, and agreed to half-day sessions once a month for the next year.

Later, Rohim reflected on how he ended up where he was. He had worked for BRAC for eight years, first as a Programme Organizer and then as a trainer. Two months earlier, he had been asked to join the Gender Team as a facilitator. He was still unsure why he was asked. One of his former colleagues said it was because he was a poor trainer and he was being punished. He didn't think that was true. He knew that Fazle Abed was a supporter of the programme, so it must be important.

He knew, too, that the programme had made him wonder about many things. It began with the training of trainers at Rajendrapur. He had really enjoyed the training, but had been troubled by the discussions about gender equality. He had not thought about gender much before those discussions. He was surprised by some of the comments his female colleagues had made. He began to think about his mother and his sisters and how they had done all the work at home. Maybe it wasn't fair. After the programme, he had started helping his wife a little with the baby. It felt good, but he knew his father would never have done it.

Now he was supposed to teach others about the importance of gender equality.

Rohim spent the next morning with the staff in the field, getting to know them and putting faces to the names on the staff list he had received from the AM the previous night.

After lunch, he began the first session, which focused on some ideas about gender and change. The TOT had stressed the importance of participation, so he was working hard to involve everyone, particularly the small number of female staff. He knew they were used to letting the men make the decisions and would need some encouragement to participate in the discussion. As he drew the meeting to a close, he sensed that people were curious about where this would go. He was grateful that he hadn't faced any angry challenges to gender equality as he had two weeks before in an Area Office near Gazipur.

Two months later, he was having trouble keeping everyone from talking at once as they argued about what issue they should choose as a priority for work. The group had first listed issues that were on their minds, then had a big argument about what constituted a gender issue. Was a tough AM a gender issue? After all, he was demanding with everyone.

Eventually, the group agreed on a list, then had to work to select a key issue. Clearly some issues mattered more to the men than to the women and vice versa. Some of the men wanted to choose overwork as the main issue. They argued it was an important gender issue because it prevented women from visiting their families. Some of the women were proposing 'women's social constraints'. Rohim brought up the criteria the GQAL programme[4] used for selecting a gender-related issue, which seemed to sway the group towards choosing 'women's social constraints'. They then drew a web diagram that analysed the causes of the issue and the causes of the causes. Ultimately, they had a map of causes and had selected three 'actionable causes':

- BRAC has no policy on men being supportive of women colleagues.
- Men don't know how to be supportive of women colleagues.
- Villagers don't understand BRAC's culture and goals.

The group felt proud of their accomplishment, and after the session a few staff told Rohim how much they liked being part of the discussion. They had never previously participated in meetings in which they had been asked for their opinions on either personal or work issues.

The AM still wasn't convinced, however; he thought the meetings were a lot of gupshup (gossip) and should be shorter. Rohim agreed that it took some time, but emphasized that the Training Division had insisted the facilitator must complete the full length of the sessions.

As he left Rajshahi, Rohim reflected that the training was going well. The AM was a bit difficult, but he had worked with others who were quite supportive. He thought that it would be important to choose good actions at the next meeting and that perhaps the AM would come on board when he saw some results.

Mostly, he was looking forward to getting home to his family. He had been away for almost two weeks. He had been sick from the water in Dorshana but was feeling better now. He felt he had earned his salary this month!

The following month, Rohim had the group divide into smaller groups to discuss possible actions to address the issue they had identified the previous month. The groups generated a number of actions that usually began with 'BRAC should ...'

Rohim reminded staff that they could make recommendations to Head Office, but they also had to come up with actions to take themselves. They went back to their groups and eventually agreed that they wanted Rohim to communicate to Head Office that married women should be transferred less frequently and that, in this office, the men should support the women more in their work in the field. Moreover, the men promised they would stop teasing the women. Rohim was encouraged by this last action, and observed that, over the months they had been meeting, the men were paying more attention to their female colleagues' ideas and treating them with more respect.

Two weeks later, Rohim was at the monthly facilitators' meeting. Many of his fellow facilitators had become good friends and he found the meetings quite helpful. There was usually lots of time for the team members to raise issues they were facing and to hear others' ideas.

Rohim decided to ask about his difficult AM. A number of his colleagues had suffered similar experiences. Rohim explained that most of his AMs were supportive, but this guy was really difficult. Rohim's colleagues told him he was doing the right thing by continuing to talk to the AM about the benefits of training for the office. 'Tell him about how many of the other offices in GQAL are working more like a team,' one of his colleagues suggested. Sheepa, the leader of the Gender Team, asked Rohim if he would like a senior facilitator to talk to the AM before his next visit, but he declined. He was just happy that he wasn't the only one facing this problem. He appreciated the reassurances of his colleagues and felt more confident after the discussion.

It was not until almost the end of the year when the AM told Rohim that the programme had not been as bad as he thought it was going to be. The staff were helping each other out more, so more was getting done. During Eid, 11 out of 25 staff went home for a holiday, but there was no negative impact on loan realization or disbursement. This level of flexibility and co-operation was very unusual for an Area Office. The staff said it was possible as they helped each other and had become a strong team.

The women staff were also happier, because they could take a rickshaw now when they had to pass the market where they had been harassed while riding their bicycles. Staff were also very satisfied that relatives of female colleagues were now welcomed and entertained when they visited their wives/daughters/sisters at their workplace. They felt less embarrassed, as they had built separate toilets for women and men.

Rohim was happy things were working out in the office, but he acknowledged, 'This might be important, but it isn't easy.'

GQAL in Area Offices

The GQAL Programme was expanded after the pilot scheme, with 900 staff in 36 offices to cover all Area Offices that included multiple BRAC programmes (Rural Development, Health and Education). Eventually, approximately 16,000 staff in 800 offices undertook at least one cycle of GQAL training.

Each Area Office had two to three action-learning teams, each of which chose to focus on different issues. The bulk of these issues related to collegial decision-making (such as women's lack of participation in decision-making), management issues (such as heavy workloads and lack of time limits on work) and staff relationships. Some teams focused on programme and Village Organization (VO)-related issues, such as the non-profitability of some income-generating activities and encouraging village men to value the work of women VO members.

Although the teams chose big issues, they ultimately worked on small, actionable causes of larger issues. While the larger problems had not been solved six years later, by 2000, even taking small steps towards dealing with them meant many problems were significantly diminished.

Funding GQAL

Existing staff development budgets were used to cover the costs of GQAL. Because the sessions took place in Area Offices, the major cost to staff was travel for the facilitators, who were drawn from within the Training Division of BRAC. The costs of the external consultants were covered by a grant from the Ford Foundation.

Discontinuing the programme

The GQAL Programme continued until 2003. There were multiple reasons for discontinuing it. First, there was a feeling of saturation, as by that time almost 90 per cent of field staff had participated in the programme. Second, it was around this time that GQAL's leadership structure changed, and the programme devolved responsibility to Area Managers. The quality of the sessions declined as the Area Managers lacked the training, time and, in some cases, inclination to facilitate the process. BRAC was also beginning to experiment with implementing GQAL among VO members. These factors, combined with an ambivalence regarding GQAL among many managers, led to a suspension of the GQAL Programme. The Gender Awareness and Analysis training course did, however, continue.

Over time, as longstanding BRAC staff left and new people arrived, there were fewer and fewer field staff who had participated in GQAL. By 2014, only 5 per cent of field staff had any experience of the programme. Yet, various research projects conducted in the last decade provide strong indications that changes in gendered power relationships have persisted within BRAC.

The GQAL review process

There had been discussions about a possible review of the GQAL experience for some time, but it was several years before this review materialized. Finally, in 2012, Sheepa Hafiza, the Director of the Gender Justice and Diversity (GJD) Division, convened a meeting of ex-GQAL facilitators to reflect on their experiences. They were very enthusiastic about the discussion and shared their findings with Dr Mushtaque Chowdhury, the Vice-President of the Board. Sheepa and Mushtaque both felt that, despite the significant positive changes the programme had generated in BRAC, there was little systematic documentation of the programme to demonstrate what it had achieved and why, what it had not achieved and why not, as well as which changes endured and which had faded away. Both leaders felt that BRAC's new cohort of managers and staff had little or no experience engaging with issues of gender equality and organizational change and working in concert to generate, test and incorporate more gender-equitable values and norms into BRAC's systems and culture. An initiative on 'culture change' was happening within BRAC, but it did not draw on any of the lessons of GQAL, and did not incorporate gender issues. Yet, both Sheepa and Mushtaque felt that these issues remained highly pertinent to the effectiveness and efficiency of the organization. Their stance was supported by BRAC's founder and Chairperson, F.H. Abed.

This led to conversations between Sheepa and Aruna Rao and a concept note for a major review. Sheepa and Aruna then met in New Delhi with

Dr Muhammad Musa, the incoming Executive Director (ED) of BRAC, in November 2014. During this meeting, Sheepa and Aruna shared the lessons of GQAL and suggested how they might inform Musa's priorities when he took over as ED. Sheepa also sought the support of S.N. Khairy, Chief Financial Officer, who was employed in BRAC during the period of GQAL. Ultimately, there was enough senior support to launch the review.

That decision led to a wide-ranging analysis of GQAL and, ultimately, to this book. Below, we describe the methodology through which we gathered information on the GQAL Programme and the responses of participating staff. We adopted a multi-method approach, which included an extensive document review, interviews with senior managers and GQAL participants, workshops with GJD Team members and representatives of local communities, and a survey of a random sample of GQAL participants still employed by BRAC. The research yielded consistent results across the data sources.

Document review

A thorough document review was conducted to generate a complete picture of GQAL and identify results of the programme. This review consulted archival records for GQAL; reports done for management at the end of the pilot phase in 1996; Research and Evaluation Division (RED) evaluations and external studies; documents relating to spin-off programmes from GQAL; and relevant programme proposals and monitoring reports.

Interviews

Thirty-two GQAL participants, facilitators and BRAC staff who were Area and Regional Managers of the field programmes during the period GQAL was being implemented were interviewed. In interviews, they were asked to recall what they remembered of GQAL and to give their opinions on the results of the programme (see Appendix 2). Staff from the Gender Justice and Diversity (GJD) Division interviewed ten additional GQAL participants in the Pabna region to see if there was any variation in the responses to GJD interviewers in comparison to those carried out by the consultant.

In addition, Sheepa Hafiza and Aruna Rao interviewed senior managers who had been with BRAC in the 1990s to record their assessments of the impact of GQAL. In all, 41 people were interviewed. The list of interviewees is included in Appendix 3.

Survey

Hasne Ara Begum of the GJD Division and Rumana Ali of the RED supervised a survey of 506 BRAC staff (138 women and 368 men) who were randomly selected from the 1,700 staff who had participated in GQAL and were still employed by BRAC. The survey (see Appendix 4) asked participants to recall how useful they found the elements of the GQAL training at the time; which concepts they continued to find useful; and what they thought the impact of the programme had been on BRAC. This survey was carried out by RED, rather than the original GQAL leadership team, to reduce any possibility of bias.

Workshops

The first workshop was conducted with GJD staff. GJD also organized two half-day workshops with a cross-section of peri-urban community participants in the GQAL Programme, to hear from them about any changes they experienced through the programme carried out in communities. Finally, two workshops were conducted with staff who had participated in GQAL. Chapter 4 discusses the results of the community GQAL initiative.

Research findings

In general, staff who participated in GQAL agreed that the programme marked a significant and positive watershed for them and for BRAC. Respondents were able to recall, in remarkable detail and with great consistency, both the content of the training and the effect it had on them and their colleagues, and on the organization as a whole.

We explore these and other findings below, starting with the survey results of BRAC staff who were part of GQAL between 1995 and 2001. The first finding was that *the overwhelming majority of respondents believed that the programme was effective in changing how people worked together.* When asked to recall whether the action they took as a learning group persisted, the overwhelming majority felt that it became the usual way of working (see Table 3.1).

When asked what aspects of GQAL training they felt were most important, women rated all aspects highly, but 96 per cent marked 'Understanding women and men in our society without falling into harmful stereotypes' as the most important. The second most highly rated contribution of the

Table 3.1 Effectiveness of GQAL

Effectiveness rating	Subtotal	Number of women	Number of men
Did not work	12	3	9
Worked for some time	33	7	26
Solution became the usual way of working	459	127	332
Cannot remember	2	1	1
Total respondents	**506**	**138**	**368**

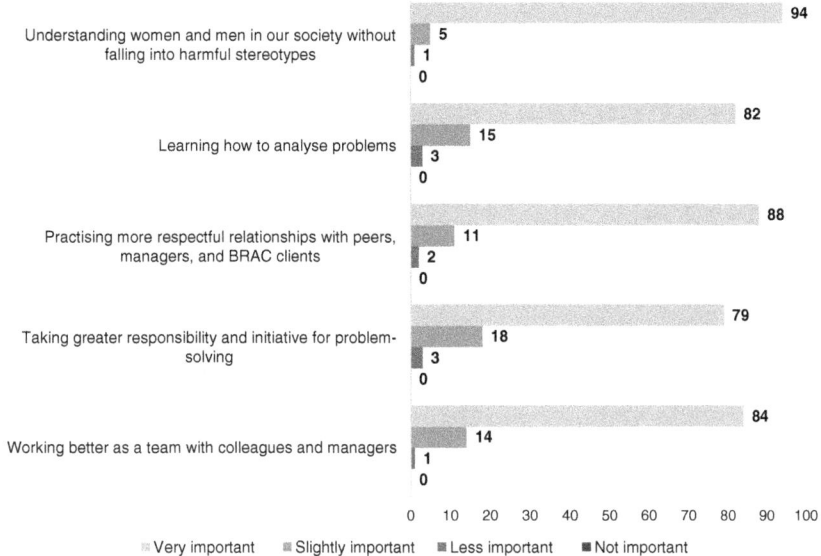

Figure 3.3 Women's opinions of aspects of GQAL

programme was 'Improved relationships (among men, women, colleagues, managers and BRAC clients)'. These were closely followed by 'Taking responsibility for and improved skill in problem-solving'. See Figure 3.3 for more details.

Men rated the importance of all aspects similarly to women; they also gave the highest rating to 'Understanding women and men in our society without falling into harmful stereotypes' (see Figure 3.4).

To assess GQAL's impact, we selected four outcomes that had come up in interviews and in previous studies of the programme:

1   Encouraged me to take responsibility for problem-solving.
2   Permanently changed how I worked with others.
3   Developed my problem-solving skills.
4   Changed my ideas about what women and men can do.

Approximately 75 per cent of the women surveyed indicated that GQAL had impacted them 'to a great extent' in each of these areas. See Figure 3.5 for more details.

As Figure 3.6 demonstrates, men were even more emphatic than their female counterparts about the programme's impact.

The final question invited survey respondents to submit additional comments. Participants gave numerous examples of how they and BRAC had been affected by GQAL action learning, which was echoed in the interviews and in the studies by Hafiza (1998) and Ghuznavi (2008).

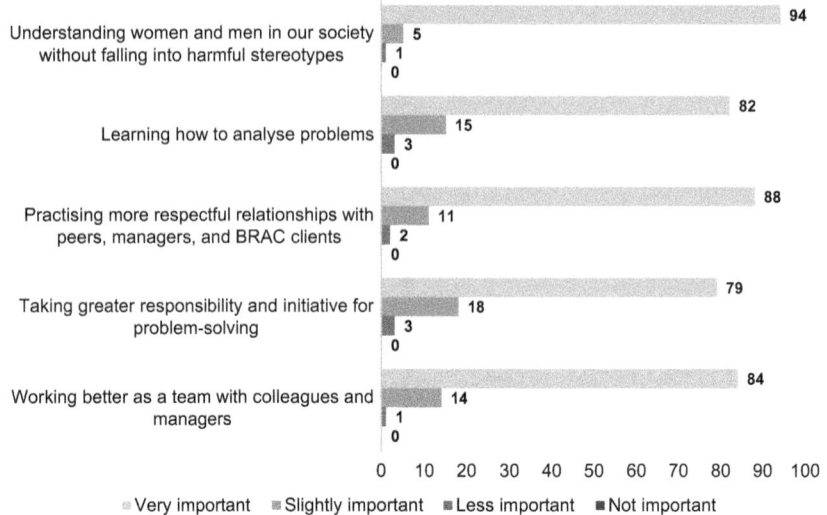

Figure 3.4 Men's opinions of aspects of GQAL

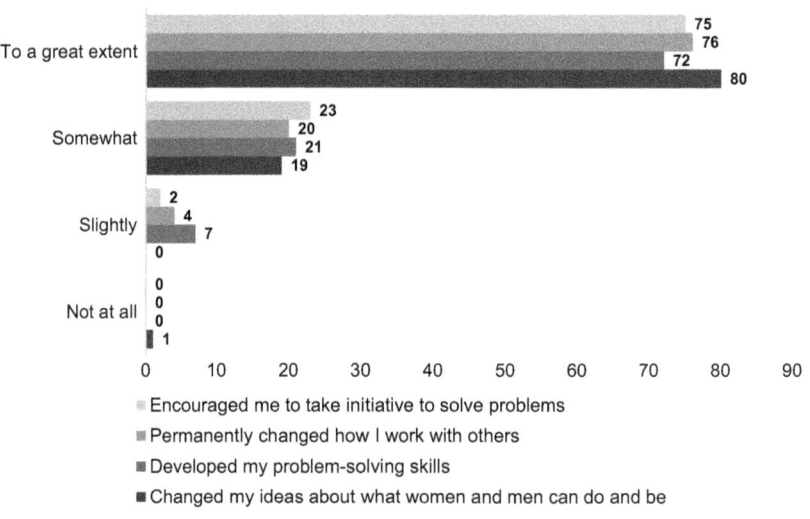

Figure 3.5 Women's opinions of the impact of GQAL

The typology of their responses is captured in Table 3.2.

Taken together, the survey data paint a remarkably consistent picture of the importance and impact of the programme. GQAL clearly inspired reflection and supported changes in staff attitudes regarding what we would assume were deeply held understandings about gender and the place of women in Bangladeshi society.

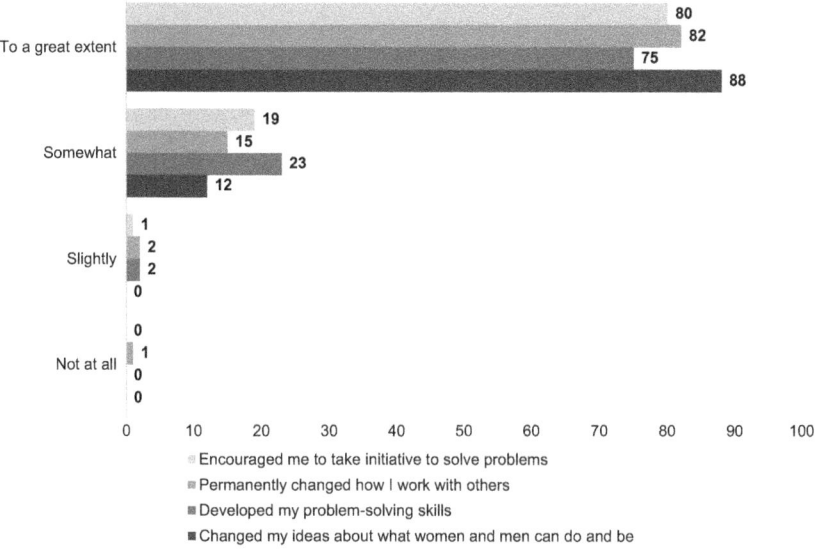

Figure 3.6 Men's opinions of the impact of GQAL

Table 3.2 Typology and frequency of changes introduced by GQAL

Type of change	Number of examples cited by respondents
Congenial work environment established through improved gender relations	203
Learning about the importance of equality between men and women	146
Positive impact on personal and professional life	297
Staff's overall skills and capacity level increased	47
Impact on policy level	32
No change	2

The interview data amplify these findings and give us a sense of what concepts like 'Congenial work environment through better gender relations' mean on a day-to-day basis. Farhana's story, below, describes the early steps towards establishing a different climate between men and women.

Farhana's story[5]

Farhana was proud she was working for BRAC as a Programme Officer. She had recently graduated from university and had wanted to be a development worker from early in her degree course. She knew it would not be easy;

there were not many women with university degrees working in rural areas and her parents had been concerned about her working away from home. It was very much against the social norm for women like Farhana to live away from home and work with poor people. Her parents were worried about her security and about the potential for harassment and abuse. They were also worried about how difficult it would be to find her a husband.

She had started working in an Area Office near Jamalpur. The hours were long and the living conditions were more difficult than she was accustomed to, but this was the life she had chosen and she was both determined to make it work and proud to be part of the development of her country.

Lately, however, she had been wondering if her parents were right. Maybe this wasn't a job for a woman. She was still angry about a recent incident. One of the male POs, who was younger than her, had told her that she didn't belong there. He said, 'Women are only good for staying at home and having children.' Some of the other male POs had also not been very friendly towards her or her friend Rehana, who had started in the office about a year before. Rehana had once engaged in a shouting match with Hassan, a senior PO who had joined villagers in teasing her for riding a bicycle.

One morning, while Farhana was in the village, she heard that someone had come from Head Office to do training about gender. She was quite surprised and curious. The programme was called Gender Quality Action Learning (GQAL). Apparently they would meet for a training session every month for a year. The first session included staff from all levels, including the Area Manager, and was about how men and women were different and whether these differences could be or needed to be changed. She and Rehana were in a small group with Reza, a programme assistant. The groups were asked to make a list of the ways in which men and women were different. Later, the facilitator asked the group whether these differences were biological or could be changed. There was quite an interesting discussion and a lively debate.

Although she and Rehana hadn't said anything during the discussion, later they wondered together: was it really true that women could be promoted like men? They also wondered about something the GQAL facilitator had told them after the meeting. He said that they should speak up in the meetings and that women had as much right to speak as men. Farhana had disagreed, saying that men should be the decision-makers, but Rehana wondered if it might be true that women could speak up and participate in decision-making.

The next two sessions were devoted to more discussions about gender issues in Bangladesh and what it would look like if gender relations were equitable. They also discussed the change process and heard stories of how other offices had approached addressing gender issues. Then the facilitator told them that they could contribute to the kinds of changes they had been discussing by selecting an issue they could work on in their office. The facilitator asked them to write issues on a sheet of paper and reassured them that nobody would know who wrote what.

Farhana hesitated for a long time before writing anything; she had thought of how things could be better, but she wasn't sure. She noticed Rehana wasn't writing anything, but Aisha was. Eventually, Farhana wrote down something she had been thinking about since the first session: the men ate first and received more food. She knew that this was similar to the practice in many Bangladeshi families, but as they were all doing the same job, it didn't seem fair. She wrote down her point and handed it to the facilitator with a combination of excitement and trepidation.

As it turned out, the issue of food had been mentioned by other people as well. The facilitator listed all the issues staff had raised and then proposed a set of criteria with which to judge which issue to work on. After much discussion, the group selected 'Not enough time for family'. This was important for Farhana as it had been many months since she had seen her relatives. She realized that this was a gender issue but addressing it would be good for the men, too. She was disappointed that her issue hadn't been chosen but proud of herself for writing it down and gratified that others had raised the same point.

Interviews with managers and GQAL participants revealed their understanding of the changes associated with GQAL. For example, one manager (later a GQAL facilitator) recalled:

GQAL was a successful programme. Among other things, the culture of meeting together and sharing was an important one. There was also a focus on gender issues related to the staff. This was due to a shift in perspective about women. Women were not treated as merely 'women' any more. There was no reluctance to recruit women as managers any more, while the situation was quite the opposite earlier. In the office, mentioning certain things as 'women's work', such as serving food [and] entertaining guests, had been stopped as well. Women used to be teased as 'girly' and male colleagues often made remarks such as 'You have GQAL, we can't say anything to you now; if we do, you will tell it in the GQAL session.' They stopped making those remarks after GQAL.

The official hierarchy had also eased up. Earlier, they could not talk with the managers easily, as there was some hesitation and fear. Later, they could. Riding a motorbike was mandatory for the branch managers and it was the reason many women left their jobs, but that was changed later. Guest rooms had been set up for women so that their families could visit. Later, staff could request postings closer to their native districts and even spouses could work either in the same office or in offices near by.

Also, because of my involvement with GQAL, I succeeded in promoting gender equality in my family. Even after leaving GQAL, when I worked with schoolchildren, I could teach them about the importance of gender equality and they changed their behaviour accordingly, which was very gratifying.

The lack of faith of the staff on the potential for change was the biggest obstacle to GQAL's implementation. Staff could not believe that any change could take place in BRAC. The attitude of male managers was also a big problem. They thought it was a matter related to the women only; if they did not attend the sessions it would not be a problem. This attitude was the most important problem.

The biggest weakness of GQAL was that it could not reach the higher management of BRAC. If it were implemented in the Head Office along with the field offices, it would have been better. They [higher management] would have understood the issues better.

Another interviewee, a female GQAL facilitator, related the story of one of her GQAL facilitator colleagues and how the ideas in GQAL spilled over into her family life:

Her memorable experience about GQAL was about a couple working in the same office. The wife used to complain to her about her husband, as he did not take any responsibility in the household. She would ask what training could be provided to change her husband. The facilitator consoled her, saying that change would take place with time. At the later stage of GQAL, that lady came back to the facilitator and said, 'I have no words to thank you! My husband used to return from work and go out to hang around with his friends, taking no responsibility and not helping me at all in household tasks. I had to do all the chores alone and look after the kids, though we both returned home from work at the same time, doing the same work. He has now changed so much; he does not go out after work and either he takes care of the children or helps me with household tasks.' She could not stop her tears. The facilitator said that it had been very gratifying and memorable that she could change at least one person.

Another interesting incident took place in her own life. Her husband was a lazy person. He did not do any household tasks; for example, he did not hang the mosquito net or even pour himself a glass of water – instead, he asked her to serve him. After starting work as a GQAL facilitator, she realized that she was doing so many things to change people while her own household remained unchanged. This irritated her. She was looking for a solution but she could not broach the subject, as her husband might have resisted. She was searching for a 'soft' way to deal with it. Then, she gradually started to do very tiny things persistently to change his habits, such as when he asked for a glass of water she started to give him the jug so that he could pour water in the glass himself; or, after hanging the mosquito net, she would ask him to tuck in the loose ends. She also shared stories about GQAL with him, and about the other staff, so that he could realize how he acted in comparison and change. It worked and he started to change slowly. Later, he even started to help her in the kitchen, cooking or preparing food. She believed this was the result of GQAL.

These positive responses from GQAL participants seem to contrast with the impression of BRAC staff that Sheepa Hafiza and Mushtaque Chowdhury formed in 2014 when they started discussions with Aruna Rao on this initiative to document the GQAL findings. They worried that, as the bulk of GQAL participants had left BRAC, the current staff had little experience in thinking about gender equality and the necessary organizational changes. This raises questions as to whether these findings describe only the experience of GQAL participants and the context of the Area Offices in the period from 1994 to 2003. It is clear from the interview data that the changes persisted among individual GQAL participants for many years. But did the programme leave a lasting mark on BRAC's organizational culture? Or did the impact survive in interstitial[6] spaces within BRAC while the overall culture remained ambivalent about gender equality? This seems possible, as only about 500 staff who went through GQAL were still in BRAC by 2014 – a small but not insignificant number in an overall staff of 43,000. We discuss the extent of the changes further in the Conclusion.

Results synthesis

In looking at all of the interviews, workshops, survey data and previous research studies, we have developed the following synthesis of outcomes and impacts.

Better working relations and mutual support in offices

The most common stated outcome or change achieved has been improved working relationships and more open communication at the Area Office level. Participants said that the facilitators encouraged them to greet each other and ask after their well-being. Even such simple practices, they said, improved the office atmosphere (2015 interviews).

For women, there is some indication that the improved relationships with their male colleagues and more cordial atmosphere in the Area Office have made staying in BRAC a more attractive proposition. For example, a female RDP Programme Assistant reported to a GQAL facilitator that she had changed her decision to resign after seeing such improvements in the office (Rao *et al.*, 1996).

In the Health Programme, which historically has had more women staff than other departments, staff cited improved working relationships between men and women and more women eating with male staff. Previously, women had eaten separately after men had enjoyed their choice of food. As noted in Farhana's story, this was one of the points raised in the discussions of issues that could be tackled through GQAL (2015 interviews). Participants reported that their issue analyses and action plans were documented on posters that were hung in the halls of the office; whenever people reverted to old discriminatory or non-collegial behaviours, they would be gently reminded of their previous commitments (2015 interviews). Staff reported that it became a matter of honour to comply with their commitments.

> In the office, cleanliness, separate toilets for women and Village Organization members did not exist and were introduced. Respect for staff such as guards and cooks, as well as for managers, increased. Staff began to greet and care for each other and took care of the sick, or [helped out] if someone was in trouble in their personal life.
>
> (Male participant, interview, 2015)

Sheepa Hafiza researched behaviour in GQAL and non-GQAL offices for her Master's thesis, and found significant differences in office culture. In offices participating in GQAL, there was better work cover when someone needed to go on leave, and permission to take leave became easier to acquire. Staff members – not only managers – took responsibility for organizing the agendas for staff meetings and contributed more frequently (Hafiza, 1998).

The relationships among all levels of staff, specifically among Programme Assistants, Programme Officers and managers, and between Area Office staff and Regional Managers (RMs), improved. RMs reported that the 'commanding voices' of managers had changed to 'listening voices' – a significant shift that suggests the development of a more open and inclusive, and less hierarchical, office culture. Some spillover effects of this improved relationship could be seen in the joint problem-solving and mutual support among staff members, and in improved time management and efficiency across teams. Staff members were more inclined to help one another, for example by working with clients when the person who was normally responsible was out of the office. While previously managers had simply issued instructions, the staff now analysed problems and tried to come up with joint solutions. The RMs concluded that there was increased staff ownership of the work – it was no longer only the manager's problem or BRAC's problem; staff also felt responsible and able to find solutions.

Another important development was that more staff were identifying pro-grammatic problems early on. This allowed problems to be dealt with before they took on larger proportions. Managers reported a greater willingness, on their part, to listen to these problems and not to penalize staff for raising them. The increased transparency among staff led RMs to report that they had more confidence that they were receiving accurate information from the Area Offices – in other words, they no longer perceived Area Managers to be filtering infor-mation for their consumption. Moreover, RMs were confident that if the Area Managers did not raise problems, the staff would.

In addition to supporting staff to take the initiative in raising and solving issues, Area Managers played a critical role in enabling the GQAL Programme to continue during the period of civil unrest that affected Bangladesh in the late 1990s. During this period of 'non-cooperation',[7] political instability and the resistance of extreme fundamentalist groups against NGOs like BRAC prohibited GQAL facilitators from travelling outside the capital. Area Managers stepped in, facilitating follow-up meetings with the action-learning teams and ensuring that the change process continued (Hafiza, 1998; Rao *et al.*, 1996).

Greater recognition among women and men that women were capable of doing BRAC work, and respect for women's contributions

The needs assessment carried out in 1994 found that just over half the staff believed women were capable of doing BRAC work, which meant that almost as many believed the opposite. Female GQAL participants described being asked to do 'housekeeping' work, such as serving tea to guests, and being told they could not do the 'tough' work of administering loans. They were not asked for their opinions; were more likely to be transferred if there was a conflict with their supervisor or other staff; and were less likely to be invited to take human resources exams (required for promotion) during the yearly performance appraisal.

Slowly, though, things began to change. For example, women staff in the Health Programme began to share the responsibility of monthly report writing, which had previously been held by men. This involvement gave women a better overview of the work done by the office and helped them to participate more actively and constructively in work meetings (Rao *et al.*, 1996). In RDP, there were some small but significant gains in building more gender-equitable relations. Male staff reported more respect for the capabilities of women staff, and in some cases went out of their way to stop community members from teasing women staff who rode bicycles or to make sure women got home safely when working at night (Rao *et al.*, 1996; 2015 interviews). A number of respondents also suggested that they no longer discouraged their women friends and family members from seeking employment in BRAC.

Women said they felt more confident and were better appreciated and respected in their offices. In one particularly telling example, a woman reported that when an RM asked if staff in the Area Office often worked late, the staff members who spoke up denied that they did. In fact, staff did often work late, especially when loans were collected and amounts had to be recorded and reconciled. Working until midnight at such times was not unusual. Remembering what they had discussed in the GQAL sessions, she gathered up her courage and explained that they all worked late because the numerous reports took hours to prepare. The RM asked her to show him these reports, and when he saw the amount of overlap and duplication he initiated a process to cut down significantly on unnecessary reporting, not only for that office but for the whole system (2015 workshops). This type of story was reported time and again.

Another spillover effect of better communications at the Area Office was improved work–family balance. Managers cited greater sensitivity to staff members' need to communicate with their families; they were more willing to grant leave on a regular basis and less likely to view this as a lack of commitment to work. RMs were pleasantly surprised that posting spouses at the Programme Assistant level in the same area or close to home had not resulted in decreased work efficiency; in fact, quite the opposite had occurred (Rao *et al.*, 1996).

Because participants were encouraged to change their attitudes and behaviour at home as well as at work – in one exercise participants were asked to do some of the chores normally done by the opposite sex – a number of men participants reported doing more of the housework. They reported taking care of children, doing laundry and arranging the mosquito nets. In the 2015 interviews and survey, respondents said this behaviour had continued in their family life.

Women gained self-confidence

During the needs assessment, the Gender Team noticed that women spoke much less than men, even when they were present in significant numbers. '*Bhai* [male colleague] has already said it, so why should I repeat it,' women told the facilitators, explaining their reticence. The Pilot Phase Report, the survey and the 2015 interviews all revealed a growth in women's willingness to express their ideas and feelings since the start of the GQAL sessions, which continued in their professional and personal lives, whether in regard to problems in the office, work in the villages, or gender relations in the home.

> GQAL changed my mindset and at the same time it helped me a lot to change others' mindsets. I learned to raise my voice for my right. It gave me the courage to speak up for others, and to talk to senior local government officers.
>
> (Female GQAL participant, interview, 2015)

Reduced harassment of subordinates and peers

Women staff talked in the GQAL sessions about how comments describing how pretty they looked in their outfits, how well their lipstick suited them and more suggestive remarks made them feel uncomfortable. They also cited examples of being asked to enter supervisors' offices for evening discussions. Both women and men talked about angry supervisors or colleagues throwing papers at them or yelling (Rao *et al.*, 1996; 2015 interviews).

Ghuznavi (2008: 8) documented important changes in men's attitudes as a result of GQAL. Significantly, she noted, 'women almost uniformly reported a reduction in various forms of harassment'. She also reported some men becoming more respectful towards and encouraging women to be part of their social interaction as peers. Some men said that the GQAL sessions had allowed them to understand that what they thought was 'just teasing' was in fact deeply hurtful and constituted harassment or hostile behaviour.

All agreed that such behaviour was unacceptable; publicizing this agreement greatly reduced such incidents.

> I see now that there was a culture of misuse of power. However, nowadays it has changed a lot. Now managers have become very accountable, especially in dealing with their supervisees. The *Mon Khule Kotha Bola* [staff forum to raise organizational issues; see below] is one result of GQAL that supports this accountability. It has the additional value of transmitting our voice to management.
>
> (Female GQAL participant, interview, 2015)

Organizational adoption of issues and solutions raised by GQAL

Although Area Office teams were primarily taking action on local issues, they were also diagnosing problems in BRAC more generally; these were carried upward by the facilitators and the AMs in regional meetings. BRAC managers supported the resolution of problems uncovered by the GQAL process. This situation convinced staff that they would be heard and dealt with fairly, and encouraged them to raise issues and address problems that had previously remained hidden. It is important to emphasize the contribution of the 'virtuous circle' that the combination of top-down and bottom-up change introduced by GQAL made to staff satisfaction and commitment, and to better overall functioning of the organization. It gave staff confidence that their voices were important and put in place formal and informal systems to address programmatic and human resource issues in a way that allowed the organization to tackle them before they developed into crises. As long as it lasted, GQAL offered feedback loops and checks and balances to prevent abuses in a fast-growing organization.

> Investigation and action on complaints of sexual harassment created confidence among the staff that action would be taken and the process was fair. It contributed to the success of GQAL immensely. Before, staff could never take any issue to higher management if it concerned their immediate supervisor, and women staff did not know about their rights. They became aware of their rights, how to raise their voice against abuse, and how to seek remedy … Many male staff never realized how their behaviour could hurt female colleagues, and they assumed their acts were benign. When they realized, they stopped. If they had not been convinced, they would not have changed their behaviour at home either.
>
> (Female GQAL participant, interview, 2015)

A good example of the mixture of formal and informal norms was the policy on 'desk leave', which gave menstruating women the right to work in the office and not do field work in locations where there were no toilets or washing facilities. This policy already existed when GQAL began, but it was very rarely operationalized. When women discovered that the policy existed, and perceived their colleagues to be more receptive to their needs, they gained the confidence to exercise their rights and ask for desk leave. Men also became aware and alert to 'walk the talk' of the policy in practice. In examining this problem, staff discovered that HR policies and circulars were often locked away in the manager's desk and therefore put into practice only at his/her discretion. When this came to light, senior management ensured any new HR policies and circulars would be read out to all staff and that the policy manual would be available to all for consultation (Ghuznavi, 2008; 2015 interviews).

Another outcome of GQAL was that management reduced after-hours work and weekend visits to Area Offices, which had been regular practices and had extended the working week for staff employed in those offices. As a result of information that emerged through the GQAL process, BRAC also developed policies on paternity leave and sexual harassment.

Another important change was in response to problems posed by transfers and leave. Sometimes these transfers were arbitrary – for example, if the manager did not like a staff member or wanted to favour a particular individual. More problematic was the fact that there was no inclination to post a person near to their marital or family residence, or close to where their spouse worked. Management believed that if leave were granted too readily, it would dis-courage devotion to work; in fact, the opposite proved to be the case. These issues were raised through GQAL, resulting in transfer and leave policy changes that were much appreciated by staff.

On the programme side, managers made sure that problems experienced by beneficiaries were addressed in a system-wide way. For example, chicken rearing was a popular income-generating activity for VO members. More thought was given to scheduling chick deliveries to avoid high mortality rates, and systems were devised to support individual women who needed emergency help to ensure their livestock were fed and/or their crops were tended. Some of the accounting processes for loans were simplified and, where possible, computerized.

As BRAC expanded, there was less and less co-ordination between BRAC programmes in a given region. GQAL facilitators noticed this and reported it to regional management and, through them, to senior management. In consequence, BRAC developed the position of the 'BRAC Local Representative', later called 'BRAC District Representative'. These representatives' role included keeping abreast of the various programmes and representing BRAC at the local co-ordination meetings organized by Government District Commissioners, as well as ensuring that the organization interacted with local authorities in a coherent way.

When issues of women's harassment and the arbitrary use of power by supervisors were raised in GQAL sessions, staff sought more guidance from

BRAC on what was and what was not acceptable behaviour. These issues raised by GQAL eventually led to the institution of a comprehensive gender policy in 1997. This policy was developed by a committee headed by Dr Salehuddin Ahmed, the Deputy Executive Director, and included the GQAL Team leader.[8] Another significant result of GQAL was the articulation of a set of BRAC values, also in 1997, which continues to be widely disseminated and supported throughout the organization. By creating space for a debate across BRAC about what these values mean in terms of day-to-day behaviour, GQAL enabled new norms to be discussed and made it more likely for them to be widely socialized and respected in the organization. Many workplaces now have similar codes of conduct or codes of ethics and value statements, but the top-down and bottom-up process that generated BRAC's values was forward thinking at the time and anchored it strongly in the organization's culture and practice.

After the staff GQAL Programme ended, there was a lack of opportunities to address staff concerns. But in 2005, when the former leader of the GQAL Programme was appointed as the first Director of HR, she institutionalized a number of mechanisms, including a sexual harassment redressal mechanism. This was the beginning of a practice of developing HR policies using a gender lens. The redressal mechanism was a formal complaint mechanism to address issues of staff abuse, sexual harassment and financial embezzlement. In 2011, following a gender audit, the mechanism was upgraded to include a high-level committee named the Sexual Harassment Redressal Committee (SHRC). The Sexual Harassment Policy (SHP) was developed with a multi-department committee following a needs assessment, during which some 30 workshops were conducted with over 800 staff. BRAC is proud of the fact that the Bangladesh High Court used language from the SHP when defining 'sexual harassment' in a landmark decision in 2009.

The Director of Human Resources also introduced sessions known as *Mon Khule Kotha Bola* (speaking from the heart). These were convened for staff to speak using an 'appreciative inquiry processes' about good practices and how to address problem areas that arose in particular offices or programmes. They are still much valued by staff, and deal with a wide range of issues, organizational change processes, programme development, values, ethics and gender issues. Both staff and managers can ask for such a session to be organized. When they deal with gender issues, sessions are often held for women and men separately and they do not mix staff levels; in this way, staff can speak freely. Between 6,000 and 8,000 staff participate in at least one of these sessions in any given year. This mechanism has been institutionalized – an example of continuous policy improvement.

Increased skills for BRAC staff and trainers

From the *BRAC Technical Manual* (Stuart *et al.*, 1997: 165), it is clear that

> action-learning team members with the help of a trained facilitator are now quite familiar with the action-learning process initiated by GQAL

– they can identify and analyse an issue; develop an action plan to deal with it; and carry out a set of activities aimed at achieving their objective. This has led to increased transparency of issues and decisions taken to deal with them. The entire process was carefully shepherded by the GQAL facilitators, many of whom have evolved from trainers to change agents facilitating problem analysis and resolution. They learned skills to continually engage staff in discussions rather than confrontation through the astute use of open-ended questions and constructive engagement.

Managers who were wary of GQAL at the start were relieved to see problems resolved rather than accumulating on their shoulders, along with blame, and jeopardizing their career prospects in BRAC.

BRAC staff who participated in GQAL also became much more aware of discriminatory social and organizational norms and ways to interrogate them. For some, this was life-changing; it changed the way they approached their work, their family relationships and their friendships. They learned the power of breaking their silence, a practice that had been driven by fear, and how to create safe space in which to do so. In the 2015 interviews, participants gave examples of how this has been applied in training staff and working with young people in communities.

> We came to learn that the existing backward condition of women was due to socio-cultural norms and values, and when we internalized that realization, we started changing ourselves and started discussing with others about these issues.
>
> (Female participant, interview, 2015)

They also looked back on their role with pride. Whether they are still in BRAC or have moved to other organizations, there is still a sense of team spirit. A concrete example of this is their willingness to support people and reach a collective judgement.[9] Earlier, we described how the GQAL process helped participants to avoid either/or thinking about power as a zero-sum or a win–win game, and to take care in identifying what characterised a situation to enable the group to reach a 'fair' decision. Often issues, such as gender power dynamics, became polarized; the ability to reframe them was immensely helpful in coming to workable solutions. This was clearly the case with working relations between women and men in BRAC, and could be helpful in addressing other contentious and complex issues facing the organization.

Limitations of staff GQAL

Greater focus on internal issues rather than programme issues

There was little focus among the action-learning teams on empowerment-related issues concerning village women's groups. The teams focused on office-related issues because these were common to men and women staff and they prioritized them. The facilitators were also primarily focused on staff issues. As the GQAL Team leader said, 'we were interested to see that the staff be empowered to facilitate empowerment at the field level with the VO members, but there was no clear picture of expected outcomes of that thinking' (GQAL Team leader, personal communication). Perhaps more importantly, this process was unprecedented in that it opened the space for staff to raise their concerns: the gender space became a lightning rod for many issues of power to surface, and it became hard to override the overwhelming desire of staff to address these issues.

As most of the thinking done by the GQAL Team was focused on staff issues, it is not surprising that the facilitators did not have a clear approach to change in the VOs. Some facilitators believed that developing a plan for work with the VOs was beyond their remit and would require management approval. In retrospect, it was important that BRAC first demonstrated that it respected staff concerns (the very staff whom BRAC must depend on to facilitate steps towards women's empowerment in the villages) and modelled a process which allowed silenced voices to speak. Without this, staff would have been unable or unwilling to make the required leap towards catalysing change at the village level.

When staff chose to focus on gender issues facing village women, they did not venture far beyond existing operating procedures. For example, one Area Office team chose to focus on the issue of men's poor valuation of women's household contributions and their participation in BRAC-organized groups. To deal with this, staff lectured male relatives of village women members in 'issue meetings' on women's contributions and exhorted them to value women more.[10] Clearly, these village men's behaviour was rooted in biased gender ideologies and rigid gender roles and power relationships, and exhortation was unlikely to change that.

While staff intuitively understood this dynamic, they were unable to break the mould in finding ways to uncover such barriers and deal with them more effectively. This is not surprising, since there was not much in their experience, either educational or professional, that would have prepared them to innovate and move beyond given parameters. Moreover, people were not looking beyond target achievement to changing power dynamics because they did not know how to do so, and they were not told that this was a priority. At the same time, the rapid expansion of the RDP and the demands of loan recovery prevented the staff from focusing on newer behaviours and actions, learned in the GQAL Programme.

This stands in contrast to the community GQAL, MEJNIN and other gender-transformative programmes, as we explain in the next chapter. These programmes gradually accepted the learning from field staff and institutionalized innovation and learning in their programme design, implementation and monitoring.

Seeming invisibility of gender

In the RDP particularly, managers asked, 'Where is gender in GQAL?' This question was prompted by the choice of issues that staff prioritized, which seemingly were not 'gender issues'. Issues of power and authority, and others concerning working and living conditions within BRAC, were not seen a gender issues. These managers were not alone in wondering why we seemed intent on focusing on 'management' issues: friends in government and academia asked the same question. The GQAL Team tried, with some success, to show how these issues *were* gendered – that is, how they impacted men and women differently because of gender roles and gender power dynamics. But we faced an uphill battle in trying to make this argument as well as criticism afor going beyond our remit.

The seeming invisibility of gender is also a function of the very small number of female staff in RDP: in some Area Offices, there were no women at all, and in the remainder there were at most two or three. In contrast, the Health Programme Area Offices often had gender parity in staff, making it both more possible and more relevant for overt gender issues to surface.

Addressing issues that staff prioritized, even if they were not seen as 'gender issues', had a positive impact, because staff saw that the process dealt with their concerns and in this way it built their ownership of the process and its outcomes. It also made gender-equality issues legitimate for staff to raise, just like any other issue about which staff were concerned.

Unequal managerial support

The leadership and drive for the GQAL initiative clearly came from the Executive Director. In addition to his ongoing concern that gender equality was an important and unfinished agenda in both BRAC and Bangladesh, he wanted to experiment with different management styles and organizational cultures. As discussed in Chapter 2, the dominant style in BRAC was a top-down, 'do-as-you-are-told' model that resembled a patriarchal family or even a military hierarchy, particularly as the organization grew larger. This model was culturally familiar and acceptable to most managers and staff, but GQAL offered a different way of operating. In the staff survey, 85 per cent of respondents said that their managers supported GQAL, but in the interviews the lack of managerial support was expressed more strongly.

Probing this difference in response indicated several different patterns. Clearly, most managers at the area, regional and headquarters level felt that GQAL demanded a lot of time that could be more usefully spent on achieving BRAC's programming targets, and they were happy when the round of action learning concluded. A significant number of middle managers were not very involved in the programme. They reported that because they did not consistently receive a clear signal from their senior management to engage in GQAL, they found it hard to devote time to it and maintain an overview of it, much less master the issues and skills with which their staff were grappling. They did not actively oppose GQAL, but they were not advocates. For the most part, their involvement was sporadic, and, to some extent, the GQAL Team and some participants misread this as resistance. Clearly, some of the participants would have preferred to continue with some form of action learning after the round of GQAL, or some form of 'refresher', as a number of survey and interview respondents explained.

Some managers *did* oppose GQAL and, where possible, cut it short. However, a third group became positive supporters and advocates, and changed their own management style to incorporate GQAL bottom-up/top-down approaches. They spent a considerable amount of time with participants and consequently understood and employed GQAL approaches.

Unavoidable external and internal constraints

There were cases of excessive transfers, especially of Area Managers, in and out of GQAL areas. New staff, especially managers, entering a GQAL office part-way through the cycle slowed down the process, but did not prevent the action-learning teams from accomplishing at least some limited goals.

The disruption to GQAL caused by the non-cooperation movement (political unrest related to upcoming parliamentary elections in March 1996) and by floods in Pabna in August 1995 hampered implementation during the pilot phase. The RDP asked GQAL not to work in some of the worst-hit flood areas; as a result, the team lost a month's work in those regions. The GQAL facilitators did help with the distribution of relief supplies, which was appreciated by staff and managers. The non-cooperation unrest coincided with follow-up meetings planned for team action planning. Similar unforeseen external events continued to affect implementation after 1996.

Lessons learned

A number of factors that were critical to the success of GQAL were related to the process itself, while others related to the ability of the team to secure leadership support (which itself reflected, to some extent, the strategy of 'political knitting'):

- It was a field-based learning intervention, which was followed up regularly by trained facilitators; and its methodology was innovative and carefully constructed and tested in a BRAC field-level context.
- The process and the issues it dealt with captured the attention of staff and facilitated their ownership of both.
- Because women and men had to agree on problems that were of interest to both, the issues chosen often had greater effects on women but impacted on men too, such as: frequent transfers; the ability to take leave; and respectful and polite relations in the office and with clients. Positive changes therefore often had a profound effect on women but were supported by men, as they also benefited.
- The GQAL Team leaders worked closely with senior managers to build areas of agreement and ownership and negotiate programme spaces and

issues. Simultaneously, the programme's facilitators worked closely with mid-level managers in the field to negotiate specific programme directions through discussion, questioning and analysis of differing perspectives. When issues arose where management action could be helpful, senior managers quickly demonstrated their support.

- Sustained involvement of Area Managers was critical to success. Some AMs were initially quite worried about what the GQAL process would uncover (following the dictum that problems are meant to be controlled, not aired and discussed). But their close involvement in the process showed that analysis can clear out the cobwebs around problems and point the way to workable solutions, which staff then implemented.
- The programme clearly benefited from the support of senior management, particularly BRAC's Executive Director, who encouraged the GQAL Team to 'tell it like it is' and take risks.
- BRAC committed significant resources to this effort: it assigned senior staff with extensive programme experience to lead it and a large number of facilitators to work in the field. For the core team, the unfailing support of the Head of the Training Division, Dr Samdani, provided encouragement to work hard and instilled a commitment to do a good job. The main additional cost of the programme related to facilitators' travel to Area Offices; while this was significant, it was less expensive than transporting Area Office staff to training centres.

The cultural changes in BRAC supported by GQAL were neither all-inclusive nor permanent, but there is sufficient evidence in the initial studies and in the more recent interviews and research to suggest it was substantial and long-lasting in addressing some of the most troublesome gender-equality and workplace problems staff were experiencing at the time. This is more than most organizational change efforts achieve, and speaks well to the robust and suitable nature of the design and implementation. It did not, however, go beyond its original parameters and continue to build a virtuous cycle of improvement, whether on gender equality or on other emerging issues of concern to BRAC. This, in large part, is due to the cancellation of the programme in 2003. Perhaps more importantly, the bulk of problem-solving was limited to Area Offices. GQAL was not undertaken by more senior levels of the organization, so managers had less stake in, mastery of and confidence in continuing the process.

Although there are very strong indications of lasting learning at the individual level, results are mixed at the organizational level. For example, the percentage of women staff is no higher today than it was in 1999, and a review of the number of promotions received by women and men GQAL participants showed that the latter were more likely to gain promotion. BRAC has, however, implemented a large-scale community GQAL Programme (discussed in Chapter 4); developed a variety of gender-friendly policies and programmes; made its sexual harassment complaints process more robust; and held regular 'speaking from the heart' sessions in which staff can raise issues of concern in a safe space. These positive changes would not have occurred without some GQAL-inspired change in the broader culture of BRAC, but it is also clear that much remains to be done. We discuss what we think would be important considerations for a renewal of efforts for organizational culture change in the Conclusion, but first we turn to an analysis of the GQAL Programme in communities.

Notes

1　The full criteria for issue selection are in Appendix 5.
2　As often as we tried to make the distinction between action learning and 'training', GQAL was always referred to as 'training' by BRAC.
3　This is a composite story based on interviews and our experience in the programme.
4　The full criteria for issue selection are in Annex 5.
5　This is a composite story based on interviews with GQAL participants.
6　Interstitial spaces are thought to be countercultural spaces within a larger culture. These spaces have the potential to be influential over time.
7　Non-cooperation was a protest tactic developed by Gandhi and adopted by political movements in Bangladesh. Typically, it would include a general strike and large street demonstrations.
8　Although the gender policy was developed in 1997, full implementation awaited the founding of the Human Resources Department in 2005.
9　The ability to come to broad consensus about divisive issues by influencing how they are framed is well described in the literature on complexity theory (Zimmerman *et al.*, 1998) and communications theory (Yankelovich, 1991).
10　Issue meetings were led by BRAC staff with VO members to discuss social issues, such as dowries and violence within families.

References

Ghuznavi, F. (2008) *From Action Learning to Learning to Act: Lessons from GQAL*, Dhaka: BRAC.

Hafiza, S. (1998) 'Bringing about Change in Gender Relations in BRAC', Master's thesis, Brattleboro: SIT Graduate Institute.

Rao, A., Kelleher, D., Stuart, R., Hafiza, S., Sultana, N., Rahman, H., Rahman, S. (1996) 'Pilot Phase Report: The BRAC Gender Program toward the Next Generation', unpublished report, Dhaka: BRAC.

Stuart, R., Rao, A., Kelleher, D., Hafiza, S., Sultana, N., Rahman, H., Rahman, S. (1997) *BRAC Technical Manual: An Action-Learning Approach to Gender and Organisational Change*, www.brac.net/sites/default/files/BRAC-Technical-Manual-Chapter_01-07.pdf (accessed 22 February 2017).

Yankelovich, D. (1991) *Coming to Public Judgment: Making Democracy Work in a Complex World*, Syracuse: Syracuse University Press.

Zimmerman, B., Lindberg, C., Plsek, P. (1998) *Edgeware: Lessons from Complexity Science for Health Care Leaders*, Bordentown: Plexus Institute.

4   Implementing GQAL in the community

In 1999, the Executive Director asked the Gender Team to extend the GQAL Programme to communities in which BRAC worked. He believed that greater support among community members for equality between women and men was needed. This programme would support BRAC in its goals of alleviating poverty and empowering poor women and men. The changes in attitudes and behaviour and analytical skill-building among men and women in the staff GQAL demonstrated what was possible, and he was eager to experiment with ways in which GQAL could be transferred to villagers. During the staff GQAL process in the Jessore region, at the request of the Regional Manager of RDP, the Gender Team also organized a GQAL-inspired process with a group of very poor fisherwomen and fishermen. After the sessions, realizing the benefits of women's participation in fish farming, including increased fish harvests, the men stopped poisoning women's pools. Male participants also committed to treating their wives with respect and refraining from using violence against them and their children. During this project, the Gender Team also noticed how neighbouring families were monitoring male violence in some households and acting as a group to protest such behaviour. The experience gave the Gender Team confidence to start working with Village Organization (VO) members.

This chapter describes efforts to take the GQAL methodology into the community and the significant results that have been achieved to date.

There have been three main phases of GQAL in the community:

1   A pilot was launched by the Gender Unit (lead by the GQAL Manager) under the leadership of BRAC's Training Division (BTD), working with VOs in four Area Offices as an initial trial in 1999–2001. Shortly thereafter, BTD and BRAC's Research and Evaluation Division (RED) jointly initiated a two-year GQAL pilot programme (2001–2003).
2   GQAL was expanded to work in tandem with the programme 'Challenging the Frontiers of Poverty Reduction–Targeting the Ultra Poor' (CFPR–TUP) in ten districts between 2005 and 2011.
3   GQAL has been implemented by the Gender Justice and Diversity (GJD) Section as a multifaceted stand-alone programme since 2012, reaching a more diverse population and using a wider range of strategies, including

campaigns to mobilize whole communities and advocacy to challenge power structures.

Each phase represents GQAL being modified, expanded and adjusted based on the BRAC methodology of piloting, evaluating and scaling up described in the first chapter. We see the experimentation with GQAL as a 'stand-alone' programme and as a component that is 'mainstreamed' into other BRAC programmes. The following sections describe the reach, strategies and outcomes of each phase in some detail. We then reach overall conclusions about the influence of GQAL as an approach to promoting gender equality at the community level. In the Conclusion of this book, we locate GQAL within community methodology and broader research and development practice, particularly in relation to emerging approaches for working to change social norms.

The evolution of GQAL in the community: concepts and practices

Looking back, Sheepa Hafiza, then Head of the Gender Unit, reflected on the factors that influenced the evolution of GQAL in the community and how it built on the thinking of staff GQAL:

> From the very beginning, our vision was for participants to be the 'change agents' ... we tried 'to hand over the stick' to them. We also knew that we couldn't support changing power relations without involving men. Our initial plan was to reach the whole community at once, through, for example, popular theatre, but this only came later. We were also really attentive to quality and the thinking inspired by GQAL with staff meant that every field visit gave us insights and challenged our own attitudes and understanding of how poor villagers were experiencing gender relations. We were convinced that to bring about transformation in gender relations it was important to understand the reality of people's lives; involve members of the community; listen and facilitate ways for them to be interested and commited to take responsibility for the change. I think this is why we tried different strategies for participation. I also had a good relationship with the Executive Director, who was willing to listen ... this opened up opportunities for me and the team to rise to the challenge and to try to do things differently.[1]

A number of key features were retained as GQAL was adapted and expanded to work with the community. In working with the community, GQAL initiatives supported the creation of 'space' for analysis and discussion of gender inequalities and power relations, particularly at the household level. A critical element of these initiatives was that women and men were brought together to explore real-life examples of gender inequality that they were experiencing in their marriages, families or communities. Where possible, we structured the

GQAL sessions[2] so there were equal numbers of women and men, including male relatives and spouses. As BRAC staff and GQAL facilitators worked with participants, they tried not to prescribe what the change would or should look like, but rather to create the space for learning through which participants would themselves become 'change agents' for gender equality. Like staff GQAL processes, community GQAL facilitators were strategic in their use of instrumental arguments to support discussions about challenging gender discrimination. One of the outcomes of the initial GQAL sessions was that participants would develop action plans that they would subsequently implement in their communities. As we explore below, as GQAL evolved, its reach expanded beyond the usual programme participants (poor women and men) to include a wider range of community members, particularly key influencers (enablers or blockers) of social norms, such as village elites and local government bodies.

One of the distinguishing features of GQAL in the community, which will become apparent throughout this chapter, was the investment in efforts rigorously to evaluate the impact of the initiatives. This reflects the overall results-oriented trend that was taking hold within the international development sector, which placed a high value on strong monitoring and evaluation systems; it is also indicative of BRAC's results orientation, described in previous chapters. Most importantly, this orientation reflects an interest in cost-effectiveness which, as we explore below, had significant implications for how the story of GQAL has unfolded in BRAC.

Over time, GQAL in the community became an integrated, multifaceted, stand-alone programme that included a number of distinct elements: more formalized 'training' using 'fit for purpose' training modules to support change agents, known as 'Gender Justice Educators'; community-level initiatives using video shows, media campaigns for awareness raising and collective action; and advocacy initiatives directed at key institutions. Yet, as this important work developed, there was less emphasis on mainstreaming GQAL as a component in other BRAC programmes. We provide an overview of this evolution in this chapter, demonstrating the influence of the key principles of the initial gender action-learning approach well beyond the early efforts with BRAC staff.

Working on gender equality and social norms at multiple levels

As noted in previous chapters, even before the introduction of GQAL in the community, the staff GQAL processes had begun to influence community-level gender relations and gender-related social norms indirectly, reaffirming the point made in the Introduction about the permeability of social norms. In other words, not only do prevailing societal social norms operate inside organizations to influence organizational culture; changes within the organizational culture can influence social norms within the community. For BRAC female staff working within communities, the countercultural aspects of women's employment in BRAC, especially the employment of married women, meant that female staff members' private lives came under intense scrutiny from community members – not to mention from their own colleagues (Ghuznavi, 2008: 19). Ghuznavi (2008: 18) observed that:

> Attitudes at the community level towards women in general, and working women in particular, have also been influenced by BRAC's activities … even during the period when GQAL was focused primarily on staff members. Exposure to the women staff members working in various BRAC programmes had a knock-on effect at the community level, gradually changing attitudes among many community members. Because women fieldworkers have now been using bicycles and motor cycles in rural areas for a number of years, villagers have become more used to – and accepting of – women exhibiting such non-traditional behaviour. Not that this came without a struggle!

There was also growing awareness among some BRAC staff that gender-related norms and inequalities within communities and households were having unintended consequences for BRAC programmes, not least in relation to the complex ways in which micro-finance was impacting on household-level gender relations and women's empowerment. Micro-finance programmes were showing clear success according to some metrics: for instance, BRAC reported high loan repayment rates among women borrowers and rising incomes in participating households. Through VO meetings, women borrowers were also connecting with other women. In the process, they were building critical vocational and financial skills and knowledge, developing their sense of individual and collective agency, and overcoming their social isolation. Yet micro-finance programmes did not necessarily increase women's influence or decision-making in the family or ensure their independent control over income earned. Indeed, in some cases, their receipt of micro-finance loans was seen to be contributing to a male backlash.[3] And the preoccupation with 'credit performance', measured in terms of high repayment rates, meant that staff were often more concerned about recovering credit than addressing issues such as domestic violence or women's control over credit (Goetz *et al.*, 1996). GQAL in the community helped to draw greater attention to the intra-household gendered dimensions of economic inequality, seeking to ensure that the women who participated in BRAC's programmes benefited as fully as possible from self-employment and, crucially, did not experience increased risk of violence as a result of their role in income-generation (Hafiza *et al.*, 2015: 337).

In BRAC's health, nutrition and education programmes, social norms related to the division of food within families, the social acceptability of child marriage and violence against women, and the division of labour with respect to household tasks and childcare prevented optimal programme outcomes in an organization that was oriented towards results. As noted in previous chapters, some BRAC programmes were even finding it difficult to reach women community members. Female villagers were often reluctant to interact with male BRAC staffers in the early days. Husbands sometimes objected to their wives leaving their homes, saying that they were violating purdah. There was a very real concern among some staff that unless BRAC placed greater emphasis on changing gendered power relations, programmes that were designed to improve women's socio-economic condition and reduce poverty were likely to fall short of their objectives (see Hafiza *et al.*, 2015: 335) and would fail to contribute to BRAC's commitment to women's empowerment. GQAL in the community (like GQAL with BRAC staff before it) responded to this concern.

Piloting GQAL in communities

Initially, BRAC's management decided to extend GQAL to members of BRAC VO borrowing groups. In January 2001, the Training Division started GQAL for VO members in four areas. But after six months managers realized that if the project were eventually to become a full programme, it should start as a full pilot action research project from which lessons could be learned for future replication and expansion (Mahmud and Mahbub, 2004).[4] The initial design was also proving too staff-intensive to be scaled up. Consequently, a redesigned GQAL pilot project, which included a new training module, was initiated by the Gender Unit and launched under the Training Division in three areas of the BRAC Development Programme (BDP/RDP) in November 2001. The Research and Evaluation Division (RED) was directly involved in this project's design, monitoring and implementation (Mahmud and Mahbub, 2004).

The main purpose of the project was to create, in rural areas, an enabling environment for women's empowerment and to improve gender relations in the family, community and the borrower VOs. BRAC aimed to change gender-discriminatory attitudes and behaviour through GQAL sessions with selected VO members and some of their male relatives. It was anticipated that what was learned in the GQAL sessions would be retained and spread in the community through courtyard meetings hosted by GQAL 'trainees' (Mahmud and Mahbub, 2004).

The pilot identified seven expected outcomes, all of which reflected aspects of creating an environment of greater gender equality at the household and village levels. These were:

1   The villagers will be able to identify areas of gender discrimination by realizing the physical and social differences between men and women.
2   Women's involvement in income-generating activities and men's involvement in domestic activities will both increase, and women's contribution to the family will be recognized.
3   Discrimination between men and women regarding food intake will be reduced.
4   There will be greater understanding about the equal rights of men and women to education.
5   There will be a realization that, as human beings, men and women should have equal opportunities to receive treatment in case of sickness.

6   There will be understanding about the rationality of joint ownership of family resources by men and women, and women's participation in family decision-making will increase.
7   Violence against women will be reduced, so that women's status in the family and society will improve.

How were these changes to be achieved?

As noted above, the pilot project was implemented in three areas which were selected to cover a range of situations with respect to gender relations and women's social position. Ulipur, in the northern district of Rangpur, was selected because of its extreme poverty, attributable to river erosion and relative underdevelopment; Senbagh, in the southern district of Noakhali, was selected as it was relatively conservative and restrictive about women's mobility and economic activity; and Dashuria, in the northern district of Rajshahi, was selected because there were greater income-generating opportunities there for women and relatively few restrictions on women's mobility. Another consideration was that the Dashuria Area Office had longer experience with the staff GQAL Programme.

The project identified as participants women VO members and their male relatives (sons, brothers and husbands) from each of the selected VOs. The GQAL component was targeted at active VO members: that is, those who attended VO meetings and saved regularly; had taken out a micro-finance loan; paid instalments regularly; and maintained VO rules and discipline. It was felt that participants matching this profile would benefit most from the GQAL Programme and would be less likely to face difficult trade-offs in their family and community related to attending the training and applying the learning to their own lives. Members selected for 'training' tended to be between the ages of 25 and 45 who were articulate and vocal and had sufficient time to attend the full sessions as well as a willingness to become peer educators and conduct courtyard meetings in their villages. In total, nearly 1,900 people participated in the GQAL sessions: 1,391 women and 466 men, of whom 231 were spouses (Mahmud and Mahbub, 2004: 5).

One of the distinct features of GQAL in the community was the investment in a more rigorous monitoring and evaluation (M&E) framework to measure the programme's impact. For the pilot, the researchers undertook a baseline study to explore villagers' attitudes related to each of the above-mentioned seven outcomes. Since they wanted to be able to identify the contribution of GQAL to the anticipated changes at the community level, they undertook studies with VOs in four different situations (i.e., creating programme groups and control groups).[5] The researchers gathered baseline data on the gender-related knowledge, attitudes and practices of nearly 1,300 villagers at the beginning of the intervention as well as during and after the GQAL Programme. Data were collected from men and women in the same household using a semi-structured questionnaire, 12 focus group discussions and Participatory Rural Appraisal methods, with discussion-based activities conducted separately with women and men (Mahmud and Mahbub, 2004).

Information from the baseline enabled the programme to identify the specific gender norms and practices that prevailed and therefore which issues of gender-based discrimination to emphasize in the training. This assessment was also used in the design of a special GQAL training manual for VO members and their partners or male relatives.

Over a series of 12 sessions, using popular education techniques, including stories, posters, role-playing and other participatory methods, groups of women and their male family members were encouraged to reflect on how gender discrimination was constituted and maintained in their communities (in relation to the outcome areas described above), and to discuss whether and how any aspects of it could be changed.

Three experienced trainers who were already involved in GQAL staff training facilitated the VO members' sessions with the support of the new manual. The GQAL 'training' component was supposed to catalyse new knowledge and awareness among female and male participants and facilitate attitudinal changes with respect to: physical and socio-cultural differences between women and men; existing manifestations of gender discrimination and gender inequality; gender division of labour; gender inequality in nutrition and food intake; gender inequality in opportunities for receiving healthcare and education; women's empowerment and access to and control over resources; gender-based violence; and women's and men's combined responsibility for reducing discrimination against women to create family harmony and a positive community environment. Achieving gender equality was presented as a 'win–win scenario' for the family and the community – a beneficial outcome for all in the long run.

Trainers were selected on the basis of their strong understanding of the contextual gender issues and their skills in applying participatory training methods. The trainers 'had to be very skilful in negotiating and managing heated and confrontational discussions between women and men' (Mahmud and Mahbub, 2004: 24). The skill level of the trainers and their ability to create safe spaces are evidenced by the discussions that involved women raising issues of oppression and discrimination in front of their husbands. In keeping with GQAL principles, 'no position could be taken'; rather, the 'process was one of identifying problems of gender discrimination and women's empowerment as common social problems and seeking acceptable solutions rather than complaining and blaming' (Mahmud and Mahbub, 2004: 24).

From the outset, it was clear to BRAC that training a few VO members was insufficient to transform attitudes and generate support in the community for improving gender relations. Therefore, a second component was built into the programme's design, akin to the 'action plan' component of the staff GQAL. VO members and participating male relatives developed a 'commitment sheet' and were invited to hang it up in their own homes and track their progress towards their intended goals. There was very active follow-up of each of the households involved in this pilot by BRAC programme staff, achieved through door-to-door visits to see if the participants were doing what they said they would do. Participants were also asked to conduct 'courtyard meetings' – *uthan boithaks* – in their villages to share their new knowledge and awareness on gender issues. Trainees were seen as peer educators, and guidance for running the courtyard meetings with village members was provided during the training sessions. Each trainee was expected to host six meetings, during which commitments to support gender equality made during the training sessions would be discussed. BRAC personnel assisted trainees in conducting the meetings and tried to facilitate the support of village elites, elderly people and men who were sceptical about or even suspicious of the training and the courtyard meetings.

What were the outcomes?

The outcomes of the GQAL pilot were evident in changes among GQAL 'training' participants and, albeit to a lesser extent, among members of the wider community. Participants reported finding the discussions interesting and lively, and reported to evaluators that their attitudes had changed over the course of the sessions. The aspect of the sessions that was most appreciated by participants (68 per cent) was the clear and vivid way the subject matter was presented and analysed, using illustrations from real-life events and situations, like a meal in which family members share scarce resources such as eggs or meat, or a daily routine that differed for women and men. One example revolved around sharing an egg in a four-member group, in which four participants role-played as a family (husband, wife, daughter and son). Each group was given three boiled eggs to share. Almost always, a whole egg was given to the 'father' and the 'son', even if a woman was playing role of a man. Meanwhile, the 'mother' and 'daughter' each received half an egg. The ensuing discussion would address questions like whether or how this was different from normal; how it felt for both the person giving the egg and the recipient; what different criteria the family members might consider for favouring one family member over another; and the reasons for and merit of criteria like health needs and status.

The role-play often triggered strong responses among participants. For some, this was the first time they became fully conscious of gender discrimination. For some women (playing the role of a man), it was the first time they ate a full egg by themselves. Across many of the activities that encompassed the GQAL sessions, participants commented that these issues were known to them, but no one had ever explained or presented them like this before. The VO members who participated in the sessions, particularly women, said that the subject matter closely reflected their everyday reality and their personal experiences of gender discrimination in the family and the community.

Several women whose husbands also attended the training reported that their menfolk had changed after the GQAL training: they had become more patient and now helped with housework, bathing children, fetching water, hanging the mosquito net and so on. One woman said, 'before the training, husbands would not pay attention if their wives asked them to help with housework, but now they listen', while a male trainee in Dashuria said, 'I now realise that it will not do if the husband considers himself a lord; both husband and wife must work together' (Mahmud and Mahbub, 2004: 15). In evaluating the pilot, the researchers observed that the main changes the training engendered in women's lives were an increased awareness about sharing work between husband and wife and a weakening of the norm that men are not supposed to do household work. Some husbands who attended the training began contributing to household domestic chores (Mahmud and Mahbub, 2004: 18).

Overall, the evaluation of the pilot concluded: 'GQAL can positively influence villagers' perceptions with respect to gender relations of power (women's decision making authority), control (women's ownership of assets) and status or prestige (recognition of women's contribution to the family)' (Mahmud and Mahbub, 2004: 23). Nevertheless, the effects of the programme on actual behaviour could not be verified so soon after the completion of the pilot phase. Another complicating factor, from an evaluation perspective, was that all households were also involved in other BRAC programmes, including microfinance. Additionally, as noted above, there was quite active monitoring, with BRAC staff conducting regular household visits. This may have influenced participants' tendency to report positive attitudinal changes.

The pilot also faced implementation challenges. Initially, it proved difficult to recruit men to the GQAL sessions and courtyard meetings. It was critical to overcome this obstacle, as the participation of women *and* men was critical to the GQAL methodology. Men feared being the butt of jokes in the neighbourhood if they participated. Although men who were selected for the training tended to be sceptical, once they attended the first session, they changed their minds. The GQAL participants reported that they found it difficult to host courtyard meetings to share what they had learned, though project monitoring data shows that about 70 per cent of the target for courtyard meetings was reached in the pilot (Mahmud and Mahbub, 2004). The monitoring data captured the quantity of the meetings, not their quality; it is possible this data masked some of the challenges participants faced. Many of the participants were illiterate and lacked confidence in public speaking and knowing how to engage with their counterparts. As poor villagers, the GQAL participants found it difficult to invite wealthier neighbours and to identify an appropriate meeting place. Another issue was that women's invitations to join the courtyard discussions were not well received by male villagers. The researchers noted that, while there was some adverse reaction to the GQAL training and *uthan boithaks* in the villages in some areas, 'the presence of men in the training increased acceptability of the training and *uthan boithaks* in the village society and in a way helped to legitimise GQAL in the community' (Mahmud and Mahbub, 2004: 25).

From the perspective of programme implementation staff, including GQAL facilitators, Area Coordinators (ACs) and BDP Programme Officers, GQAL was observed to have made a significant difference in the lives of trainees, and to have influenced community attitudes to gender relations. This was attributed to the unique GQAL process, which the programme implementation staff described as 'a process of analysis and understanding, identifying reasons for gender discrimination and gender inequality in power and control … trying to find acceptable solutions to the problems without blaming and confronting, seeing gender issues as problems for both men and women' (Mahmud and Mahbub, 2004: 20). Programme implementation staff also highlighted the positive knock-on effects that the integration of a focus on gender equality and gender relations could have for 'other BDP activities (microfinance, sector programmes), since training VO members and their male relatives, particularly husbands, in gender issues would help in the implementation of those programmes, particularly microfinance, where support of the husband is very crucial' (Mahmud and Mahbub, 2004: 20). The pilot evaluation indicated that 'GQAL training and *uthan boithaks* helped in … making men more tolerant and raising their awareness about joint responsibility for success of the activities women engaged in for poverty reduction' (Mahmud and Mahbub, 2004: 24). As one AC in the Senbag region commented, 'Since men had become more patient and tolerant, women could come out more and were easier to approach [by BRAC staff]' (Mahmud and Mahbub, 2004: 24).

Integrating GQAL in the Ultra Poor Programme

BRAC management reviewed the findings of the VO GQAL pilot, made some necessary adjustments and decided to continue the GQAL Programme in concert with another programme, then known as 'Challenging the Frontiers of Poverty Reduction–Targeting the Ultra Poor' (CFPR–TUP), which offered training and assets to ultra-poor families – that is, families who are too poor to access benefits from conventional development interventions, such as micro-finance. CFPR–TUP had also completed a significant pilot phase with good results, though programme evaluations had indicated that while the practical needs of ultra-poor women were being met, there remained some scope for strengthening interventions to address their strategic gender needs and interests (see Mahmud et al., 2012: 1; Hafiza et al., 2015: 337). This tandem programme – one of the first significant efforts to mainstream gender in a major BRAC programme – began in 2005 and was managed by both CFPR–TUP and the newly constituted Gender Justice and Diversity (GJD) Unit, under the BRAC Human Resources Division. The GJD Unit was established to facilitate mainstreaming gender equality at the organizational and programme levels, and to promote advocacy on gender equality.

The CFPR–TUP Programme aimed to address the practical needs of ultra-poor women and men for food, income, basic healthcare and shelter. The complementary objectives of GQAL were to increase women's access to household incomes and a fair share of food and other resources; promote a more equitable division of labour within the household and give women an increased voice in household decision-making; and support women to feel confident and know their rights to receive assistance in the form of training and services. In this phase of GQAL, the programme extended its reach to a wider group of participants on the assumption that the process of gender-equitable change, particularly change in gender-related social norms, necessarily requires the involvement of and positive role modelling by other community members, such as VO members and their male partners, local governance committees and village elites. According to the theory of change underpinning the GQAL components, a combination of efforts among these different actors would generate synergistic changes in support of gender equality.

What was done?

Building on the earlier GQAL approach, particular emphasis was placed on working with men as agents of change along with women and to allow male voices and views to be reflected within the overall process. Additionally, as there is empirical evidence to indicate that men respond best to messages delivered by other men, the demonstration effect of male community members participating in the training process was considered to be of the utmost importance. Within the community, selected male community members could act as peer workers advocating for change with other men (Ghuznavi, 2008: 25).

The first phase of GQAL–CFPR–TUP was implemented in two districts – Netrokona and Kishorgonj. These are both located in the north-east of the country, where the primary activity is agriculture. Moreover, both districts are within the 'haor' (backswamp) region that experiences high agricultural yields but is subject to seasonal flooding, thus increasing the vulnerability of people and livestock. With a view to achieving its objectives, the programme selected ten *upazilas* [6] in two districts to implement the GQAL Programme in 2005–2006. A total of 1,200 women and men participated in the GQAL sessions. The expected outcomes were: an increase in knowledge and awareness among the villagers about gender roles and relations; better understanding of the rationality of joint ownership of family resources among both women and men; and more female participation in decision-making in the family, thus establishing gender equality within both the household and the community (Alim, 2007: 3). CFPR–TUP worked only in the poorest and most vulnerable geographical locations, following a two-year cycle in one location before moving on to a new area. GQAL had to move along with it.

The second phase (2007–2011) expanded the programme's reach and was successfully implemented in over 50 sub-districts of 10 districts, covering 30,000 households (albeit a small proportion of the total number of CFPR–TUP households). While the primary focus was still on the ultra poor, this phase adopted a more inclusive approach, covering both poor and non-poor households, and included efforts to engage men and local elites as well as community 'influencers' for a better chance at achieving attitudinal change, given that these groups play key roles in sustaining or overcoming deep-rooted social and cultural norms. The thinking behind this evolution is explained by Sheepa Hafiza:

Even if ultra-poor family members are ready to think and act differently about gender relations in their homes, this is not possible if knowledge and know-how remain confined only to them. Gender relations and norms operate in society and without similar understanding amongst power holders in communities, the willingness of members of poor familes to promote change cannot be sustained. In the back of our mind during the design of GQAL with CFPR–TUP, we expected that these men and women would develop their own platforms to raise voices against violence against women and other forms of gender discrimination, which actually happened in later years as community members established committees and networks that continue to function independently of GQAL. I believe it was possible because of the diverse groups of people of the same community; it would not have been the case if we worked only with the targeted ultra poor. This related to the overall philosophy of staff GQAL, which is to involve everyone in an area to bring about change.[7]

A total of 3,000 men and women (equal numbers of each) were given GQAL training. The trainees were selected from the Specially Targeted Ultra Poor (STUP) component of CFPR–TUP, VOs, *Palli Shamaj* (PS), which is a combination of two or more VOs; Gram Daridra Bimochon Committees (GDBCs), who are village elites; Union Parishad (UP) members, who are at the lowest administrative level of the government; and *Shasthaya Shebikas* (SS), who are women community health volunteers. One of the expected outputs of the GQAL activities in this phase was that gender equality would be successfully promoted and mainstreamed throughout the programme, indicating that BRAC was embracing the important role and potential of GQAL to achieve its objectives related to poverty alleviation and economic empowerment more broadly.

The main programme strategies for both phases were similar to those of the VO pilot, with some additional activities to engage the wider target group mentioned above. GQAL sessions were still the main entry point and the programme identified and engaged women, men and couples from the CFPR–TUP areas as 'Gender Justice Educators' (GJEs), who committed to changing gender roles and discriminatory attitudes and to raising their voices against gender discrimination and violence against women within their own homes and in their communities. Three half-day sessions (followed by refresher sessions after 18 months) were organized with 24 participants in each group, on such topics as: areas of discrimination in women's lives; gender-based violence; the gender division of labour; and gender dimensions and practices relating to access to food and nutrition, healthcare and treatment, rest and recreation, education, mobility and access to and control of resources. At the end of the initial sessions, participants developed an action plan.

The GQAL sessions were followed by courtyard meetings with STUP members and their male relatives, with the sessions facilitated by the GJEs. These men, women and youth became the change agents, taking responsibility to redress any gender-discriminatory incidents that they witnessed and to model gender equality in their own lives and actions. For example, GQAL trainers would work with peer educators to plan how to approach a landowner whose property was used by young men as a venue for harassing female passers-by, or to talk with a couple planning to marry off an underage daughter. A key follow-up step to the initial sessions, as in the earlier GQAL with VOs, comprised door-to-door visits by BRAC staff. BRAC Programme Organizers (POs) conducted these visits, monitoring the commitments and identifying actual changes initiated at the family level and through the courtyard meetings. They employed a number of methods to collect relevant data, including observation and interviews with participants and their family members (on separate visits), as well as with neighbours.

To reinforce the role of key community influencers, there were opportunities for engaging with the local BRAC forum and other influential local bodies and actors, including those mentioned above. The methodology of GQAL was expanded in other ways too, and came to include a media campaign, including videos,[8] to build community awareness and encourage social mobilization to end gender-based discrimination and violence against women and children. The GQAL Team developed issue-based videos that the local tea shops were invited to play, and persuaded the local cable operators to show the videos while people drank tea at the stalls. This meant the videos reached people who might otherwise not have been exposed to the programme. The team also encouraged GQAL volunteers to pay random visits to the tea stalls and 'facilitate' impromptu discussions with bystanders about the content of the videos. This innovative outreach method was later employed by other BRAC programmes and by many other organizations to support their efforts to raise awareness about gender issues.

The expansion of the GQAL–CFPR–TUP collaboration into a quasi-campaign strategy presaged what happened in the next phase, particularly as GQAL began to address violence against women and girls specifically. This history reflects the continuous evolution and adaptation of GQAL.

What were the outcomes?

An external end-of-programme evaluation of the GQAL–CFPR–TUP collaboration (2005–2011), undertaken by researchers at BRAC University, found many of the same positive results as the evaluation of the earlier GQAL pilot with VOs (see Mahmud *et al.*, 2012). The research study was designed to assess the impact of GQAL interventions on perceptions about gender-related social norms, as well as changes in actual practices with respect to gender-based violence, including instances of community mobilization to address violent incidents. The study's findings are reported below in some detail, since they shed considerable light on the workings of the programme.

The researchers looked at three areas[9] in each of three CFPR–TUP districts. One area had 'strong GQAL trainers' and CFPR–TUP; the second had 'average GQAL trainers' and CFPR–TUP; and the third had just the CFPR–TUP Programme. The districts were chosen to represent the geographic and social diversity of Bangladesh. In addition to a random survey of 120 households in each of the nine areas, there were focus group discussions (FGDs) and interviews with schoolteachers, *imams* (Islamic leaders), marriage registrars, members of elite committees (Gram Daridro Bimochon Committees – GDBCs), male and female council (Union Parishad) members, businessmen, *muezzin* (cantors at the mosque), farmers, *shalishdars* (judges in the informal courts), *matbors* (local landlords), women NGO and family planning workers, and wives of elite men. In addition, GJEs, both men and women, and CFPR–TUP members and their male relatives participated in the FGDs.

The strongest gender-equality outcomes were found in those areas where there was a GQAL presence. The most visible effect of GQAL seemed to be in changing perceptions and attitudes regarding gender roles in the household (less change was noted in permanently altering the actual gendered division of labour); increasing access to healthcare and nutrition for women and girls; and increasing efforts at community mobilization around violence against women (VAW). This was especially true for the GQAL–CFPR–TUP households who participated most actively in the programme, compared to better-off households (Mahmud *et al.*, 2012: 42).

One of the main successes of GQAL activities was to break down traditionally held beliefs and practices, including the idea that all housework is the responsibility of the female members of the household, in particular the wife of the head of the household. As feminist research has long argued, the gendered nature of the public and private domains has not only restricted women's mobility but also reinforced the devaluation of housework. For women in Bangladesh, the gendered division of labour, combined with purdah norms, has translated into men's dominance in income-earning activities and the public domain. As they have been socialized within these cultural norms and practices, women often believe that men's work has more value than their own – an attitude that reinforces their low self-worth and contributes to their social, economic and political disempowerment. Even as ever more women are engaging in income-generating work, both inside and outside the home, the burden of housework continues to fall on them. The GQAL Programme has therefore attempted to shift gender roles at the household level as a critical step towards achieving gender equality (Mahmud *et al.*, 2012: 15).

Key informants and FGDs in all GQAL areas unanimously identified the GQAL Programme as the major reason for changing gender roles in the household. GQAL's *uthan boithaks*, GJE training, door-to-door awareness-raising and motivational work, and follow-up of commitments were mentioned specifically by many of the informants, even those who were not affiliated with BRAC (Mahmud *et al.*, 2012: 17). Both the GQAL training and the subsequent efforts of the GJEs were seen to contribute to improving men's attitudes towards housework and changing the gendered division of labour in the home. Importantly, the GJEs also became role models in their villages. Through

GQAL, they have been supported first to change their own behaviour and then, gradually, motivate change in other people. Even people who had not attended the *uthan boithaks* were seeing changes in the educators' households and trying to emulate them and introduce the same practices in their own homes. Men who help with housework were less ridiculed by others in the community. It was also reported that, during household visits by GJEs, some men were embarrassed to be seen as uncooperative and therefore felt compelled to help their wives (Mahmud *et al.*, 2012: 18).

Mahfuz's story

Participation in the training appears to have had a radical impact on some couples. One example was provided by Mahfuz, who described himself as a former 'alcoholic'. He said that he had been both drunk and violent 75 per cent of the time, and had frequently ended up fighting with family members. Initially, when the couple arrived at the GQAL training, the trainer had to separate them and seat them far away from each other because they kept coming to blows. However, ultimately the effort paid off.

Mahfuz described the impact of his experience with GQAL:

> As I sat through the training sessions, I slowly began to realize that in fact I was the one responsible for all of the misery in my family life. I had been blaming my wife and my children for my problems, even though I was rarely willing to do any work and would invariably drink away whatever money I earned. Despite my behaviour, I considered myself justified in beating my wife when she protested, or my children when they were crying for food. Now, however, I realized that if I was ever to have a harmonious married life, it was up to me to change.

A number of those present at the meeting testified to the fact that Mahfuz had indeed been a violent drunkard. His wife, who was also present, stated, 'Most of what he has told you is true.' Yet she and others said that Mahfuz now helps out with household tasks, such as fetching water and keeping an eye on the cooking when his wife is busy. His willingness to participate in childcare was very much in evidence in subsequent meetings.

(Adapted from Ghuznavi, 2008: 29)

GQAL areas had more success than non-GQAL areas with regard to mobilizing community members to address VAW. In GQAL areas, successful community initiatives took the form of collective action against early marriage, spousal abuse and sexual harassment; in non-GQAL areas, community mobilization around VAW was evident only in the community conducting *shalishes* (local courts) on specific VAW incidents. Additionally, in strong GQAL areas, these collective actions involved a variety of actors, including youth clubs, school committees and community elites, indicating the capacity of GJEs to mobilize other actors in the community. The GQAL Programme was seen as a major factor motivating children, particularly girls, to complete at least primary-level schooling, and it was instrumental in raising awareness through GJE training and *uthan boithaks* on issues of early marriage, verbal divorce, polygamy and taking action in the prevention or mediation of such cases. In fact, in some areas, monthly meetings were held with the *upazila* chairman and committee members, in which GQAL GJEs notified them about cases of divorce and polygamy (Mahmud *et al.*, 2012: 37).

While women in all study areas were equally likely to engage in income-generating activities, women in high-performing GQAL areas who received assets under the CFPR–TUP Programme were more likely to report improvements in various dimensions of their status and in their self-confidence, as well as improvements in gender relations in the home, compared to income-earning women in non-GQAL areas (Mahmud *et al.*, 2012: 17). Key informants, for example, reported stronger spousal relations and increased harmony as a result of sharing housework. The findings of the 2012 study and a later study on CFPR–TUP (not covering the GQAL–CFPR–TUP collaboration) present a conflicting picture, however, on whether improved relations in the home are the result of women's increased income that can be used by men to purchase assets in their name (Das *et al.*, 2013), or an outcome of the changing gender roles related to household chores, as noted above. While the programme did not show significant increased independent control over income among women, women clearly perceived men's participation in household chores in a positive light. Moreover, a GJD internal monitoring report on CFPR–TUP and GQAL found that 22 per cent of men reported handing landownership to either their wives or their sisters because they had come to understand the importance and value of a woman's contribution to the family, leading, in theory, to increased female control over assets. In these ways, we can see how GQAL changed gender power dynamics in women's favour. There was also some evidence to suggest that GQAL–CFPR–TUP increased family incomes or at least protected them from erosion as women became more able to participate in the family decision-making process, thus supporting overall CFPR–TUP outcomes.

The 2012 evaluation concluded that the skill and commitment of the GQAL staff in establishing relationships with the community at different levels was one of the key factors in determining the success of the GQAL Programme. In particular, their ability to respond to situations where an intervention was necessary (for instance, stopping early marriage and mediating/negotiating changes in gendered practices) and their ability to engage and motivate people to change, as well as to demonstrate changes through their own practices, were critical. The GQAL Programme's investment in recruiting qualified staff, building staff capacity and managing their performance paid off in improved programme results. One component of the programme's design was the

Capacity Development Forum, which involved regular staff meetings, trainings and workshops for team members to follow up on the project's activities, analyse problems and support their own capacity development.

In terms of the strategic evolution of the GQAL Programme methodology, especially in the second phase of the joint GQAL–CFPR–TUP initiative, the interest and involvement of key influencers and/or power holders in the villages had a significant impact on the GQAL Programme's effectiveness, as many of the desired outcomes depended at the very least on the tacit or sometimes explicit support of the elite as well as their leadership. Active civil society bodies, such as school committees and youth clubs, also played a strong supportive role. A broader enabling environment – including the presence and activities of other NGO and governmental organizations that mobilized and campaigned around human rights and women's empowerment, access to economic opportunities and resources, and support from power holders – as well as greater social cohesion in the community strengthened GQAL outcomes. These findings contributed significantly to the design of the subsequent version of GQAL, as we demonstrate in the next section.

Many lessons were learned from the joint GQAL–CFPR–TUP initiative. Central among these was the reaffirmation that male engagement is a key factor in addressing gender power relations, and that the involvement of a wider group of elites and other community actors (primarily male) who play a role in enabling or blocking efforts to change gender roles and gender-related social norms is crucial if these changes are to be sustained. Collective action and support from community members are important in enabling women to claim and exercise their rights.

In this phase of GQAL, the GJEs also emerged as a key change catalyst, especially in creating spaces at the local level to analyse and address contextual features that shape discriminatory social norms and practices. Through their experiences, team members realized that the programme delivery mechanisms needed to be flexible in order to adjust to local conditions, such as the interests, spread and cohesion of local elites and civil society, as well as class, religious and factional power dynamics in the community, all of which influence in complex and nuanced ways the manner in which gender-related social norms are constructed and practised. This phase also served as a reminder that gender norms and practices are dynamic and shifting in Bangladesh. This not only had implications for the indicators that were used to monitor programme impact (some programme indicators, such as 'All members of family take meals together', had become common practice and had therefore lost their relevance), but also reinforced GQAL's central premise that programme interventions can nudge and nurture the emergence of positive gender norms.

Given the emphasis on value for money in programming, BRAC evaluated the cost of implementing GQAL in tandem with CFPR–TUP. The costs of CFPR–TUP per household in 2007 and 2008 were 9,352 taka (US$117) and 12,422 taka (US$155), respectively. This included provision of healthcare, assets and income-generating support, as well as individual and collective support for households and programme management. The costs of GQAL per household in the same years were 575 taka (US$7) and 837 taka (US$10.40), respectively. However, this later declined to an average of just 361 taka (US$4.50) per household in the period 2012–2015 as geographical spread was rationalized and GQAL gained experience and increased efficiency in training and working with community volunteer GJEs.[10] These figures suggest that the GQAL Programme and its significant results were achieved at minimal cost. Nevertheless, the GQAL Programme was dropped as a component of CFPR–TUP in 2011 (for reasons that are explored below) and took a new direction.

GQAL as a stand-alone programme

During the years that GQAL was implemented as part of the CFPR–TUP Programme, a number of events occurred that culminated in the development of GQAL as a significant stand-alone programme in 2010, managed by the GJD team. The initial GQAL pilot with VOs was, of course, also a stand-alone programme in the sense that it targeted the specific needs and circumstances of women and men in VOs and operated independently of other BRAC programmes. Yet the new version of GQAL, as we see below, was conceived as a more fully elobrated 'programme', building on learning about the need for an integrated set of activities across multiple levels, both responding to and engaging with multiple stakeholders in support of gender-equitable norm change. In other words, the new GQAL Programme sought to work across all the quadrants of the Gender at Work Analytical Framework (see page 29 of this volume) in a holistic way to support gender-equality outcomes. In the Conclusion, we consider the implications (and indeed some of the contributing factors) of this move away from a strategy of integrating GQAL into other major BRAC programmes, keeping in mind that it was only in 2015 that the organization adopted 'gender mainstreaming' as a formal organizational strategy for gender equality. This strategy was adopted only after several successful pilot initiatives within education and health programmes and BRAC Enterprises had built support for the idea that integrating GQAL thinking into non-gender-focused programmes could be an effective way to promote gender equality and empowerment.

Igniting public interest in GQAL: student workshops on sexual harassment

In 2006, during the first phase of GQAL–CFPR–TUP – and entirely driven by an altruistic motivation to support change, without any financial support from other programmes – GQAL staff initiated a workshop with approximately 80 schools to create space for students to talk about 'good touch, bad touch' and sexual harassment – taboo topics at the time. It immediately became popular with students and teachers, who would wait impatiently for the discussion to start. It also drew the attention of local news media. Unfortunately, the project had to conclude after just one year as the GQAL Programme moved elsewhere, along with the rest of CFPR–TUP. The GJD Director received many written requests from parents and teachers to continue the work, but this was not possible at the time. Later, in 2008, the GJD Unit started awareness-orientation workshops in universities, focusing on sexual harassment. The positive response motivated the GJD Unit to work directly with university students in hostels and to support them in engaging in public discussions and debates about sexual harassment. Then, in 2009, local and national print media started publishing stories about sexual harassment. For example, there were cases of young female students who had been sexually harassed and then committed suicide, with these tragedies compounded by the subsequent suicides of their parents. In another part of the country, a college professor was killed as he protested against the sexual harassment of female students. A mother met the same fate. These stories motivated women and men across the country to raise their voices against sexual harassment. BRAC was among the NGOs and human rights organizations that participated in the protests. Inspired by BRAC's Chairperson and supported by all the other BRAC senior leaders, the GJD Team designed a new initiative – MEJNIN (*Meyeder Jonno Nirapod Nagorikotto*) or Safe Citizenship for Girls.

MEJNIN

MEJNIN was a neighbourhood-based campaign that used 'edutainment'.[11] It involved a range of stakeholders and was designed to generate awareness about the severity of sexual harassment and its negative impact on girls' participation in education and their right to freedom and choice. By 2015, MEJNIN included 200,000 students (40 per cent of whom were boys) and another 100,000 community members, police, journalists and so on. It used school-based student orientations to undertake mass outreach and public educational campaigns at the community, regional and national levels. It also worked closely with journalists on a media campaign and with state authorities (police and concerned ministries) to maximize its results in favour of ensuring girls' rights to education and advocating for the eradication of child marriage (BRAC, 2013).

MEJNIN's interventions were designed to contribute to the achievement of Millennium Development Goal (MDG) 3 on gender equality. It particularly aimed, through a mass awareness and sensitization campaign involving students, teachers, parents and community watch group members, to support adolescent girls in preventing sexual harassment, protecting themselves and coping with the effects of harassment. It also had a strong advocacy component and facilitated collective action against sexual harassment. Sexual Harassment Elimination Networks were formed by the various stakeholders, with some remaining active even when MEJNIN left the locality.

Evaluations of the programme reported positive results across all stakeholders (girls and boys, parents, teachers and community watch groups) in relation to change in their understanding of what constitutes sexual harassment; changed attitudes about sexual harassment as a form of violence and a crime; increased attentiveness to incidents of sexual harassment; and increased reporting of all forms of sexual harassment (RED, 2013; Gender Justice and Diversity, BRAC, 2014). Most of all, MEJNIN contributed to breaking the culture of silence around sexual harassment and made a nationwide contribution by having 'eve-teasing' (a euphemism for public sexual harassment and molestation that is used throughout South Asia) formally recognized as a form of sexual harassment that is now a punishable crime under national law.

POSITION *and the relaunch of community GQAL*

Inspired by the successes of earlier phases and learning from the experience of the programme implementation of GQAL and MEJNIN, in 2010 a new phase of GQAL was launched as an independent programme of the GJD Unit, initially under the title 'POSITION' (Enhancing a Positive Life). Two years later, the title reverted to GQAL, as this was a known brand and represented a respected approach to programming in support of gender equality. As noted above, although positive results were achieved working with CFPR–TUP, GQAL had very small programme coverage and it had not been expanded or mainstreamed by the CFPR–TUP Programme. A donor came forward to support further GQAL initiatives and, acting on advice from the Executive Director and others, GQAL started working with a much larger population as a stand-alone programme to demonstrate that change in gender relations is possible in the community. The thinking was that positive results on a larger scale would prove the value of the approach and its potential for replication within larger BRAC programmes, other NGOs and government departments.

As POSITION, the programme was implemented in two *upazilas*, accepting a new challenge by working in a complex and densely populated peri-urban and commercial location and reaching around 144,500 households. POSITION retained many of the same programme components from previous GQAL initiatives, such as supporting the development of GJEs and integrating courtyard meetings, popular theatre and videos. The programme's reach extended to a more diverse population in terms of class, enthnicity, age and locations. It also targeted 85 secondary schools, of which 34 were religious-based. Like MEJNIN, it was not co-ordinated with other BRAC programmes; rather, it worked on its own.

In the 2012 relaunch of POSITION as GQAL, the programme maintained the earlier objectives, namely: to increase the decision-making capacity of women participants on issues that affect their lives and well-being and to support women and men to work together to change gender relations and reduce VAW. In addition, in this new phase, the GQAL Programme took into greater consideration the wider context of household–community–state dynamics (Hafiza *et al.*, 2015: 338). This version of GQAL, which continues to this day, engages with different age groups and social classes – from poor rural villagers to urban dwellers – through local institutions such as schools, police, women's groups, media and legislators who favour gender equality, and also initiates joint actions with community and government agencies to promote change. As with the earlier programme, GJEs are key catalysts of change at the household and community levels, though a new role is played by youth educators in support of community-level change. The programme also has more of an explicit emphasis on engaging with boys and adolescents. A separate programme, SAMPRITI (described below), was launched to focus on women-led collective action and leadership. To date, there has been increased local-level policy advocacy by women's groups targeting local government authorities, bureaucrats and other members of the civil administration.

What are the programme's strategies?

By 2015, the GQAL Programme had reached nearly 400,000 households in 1,060 villages – a total of almost 2 million people in eight districts across Bangladesh. Each intervention unit of GQAL is a 'spot' consisting of 500 households. In each of these spots, there are five collective forums or committees. Each forum has between 90 and 100 members, who act as 'Gender Equality Promoters' to build gender equality in their communities.[12] By the end of 2015, there were more than 23,000 Gender Equality Promoters working in GQAL communities. Below, we describe the various forums in some detail to help illustrate the role these groups play in supporting the programme's objectives.[13]

SAMPRITI and the role of Gender Justice Educators

SAMPRITI stands for 'Strengthening Awareness, Mobility, Participation, Rights, Inclusiveness and Transforming Ideology'. A forum comprises 30 poor women from a single community. It aims to create a space in which women can build solidarity, develop their abilities and define their own agenda for change – all important aspects of building women's capacity for collective action and leadership. These women attend interactive discussions at least three times a week, during which they identify problems and issues they face in their day-to-day lives, analyse them and explore their root causes. The most common issues that the forums address relate to VAW, gender discrimination, abuse and sexual harassment. One objective of SAMPRITI has been to engage different government and non-government institutions and actors to ensure access to services for the members, especially adolescent girls. Each SAMPRITI member receives intensive capacity-building support in the following areas: gender awareness; gender discrimination; sexual harassment and VAW; rights and entitlements to government services; literacy; numeracy and life skills (Jahan *et al.*, 2016: 2).

SAMPRITI was established to respond to previous programme learning about the need for separate spaces to foster women's collective action and agency. Women and men are still brought together to discuss issues related to discrimination in the family and society and to work together to challenge stereotypical attitudes and practices. The women-only groups, however, give women an opportunity to build their knowledge of laws and policies that affect them and increase their life and leadership skills (e.g., by writing their names, developing their negotiation skills, participating in team-building activities, etc.). The opportunities provided by SAMPRITI also help to connect women to other women, reducing their isolation and building their self-confidence and capacity to take collective action.

As in previous versions of GQAL, a key role is played by GJEs, who are organized into forums, each of which consists of 20 members (10 of whom are spouses). The courtyard meetings remain important activities through which the GJEs and other volunteers share their learning with the wider community. The key issues and messages of the GQAL Programme – which relate, for example, to equality in access to food and nutrition; education; domestic violence; and access to health services and other resources – are discussed in the courtyard meetings. These often include visual aids and pictorial pre-sentations and follow a sequence that begins with gender discrimination at the family and community levels. The discussion then moves on to explore the adverse effects of such discrimination and the positive effects of non-discrimination, with concrete action points identified to stop discrimination. Finally, the participants openly and collectively commit to follow the action points. These courtyard meetings are often supplemented by video shows and popular theatre in the communities (media spots) and household visits from the GJEs.

To give one example, the negative effects of malnutrition – which some-times results from unequal distribution of food at the household level – are discussed in these forums. Participants pledge that they will ensure a balanced diet and equal access to food for all household members. The participants dis-cuss their learning among themselves as they continue to chat outside the courtyard/SAMPRITI meetings. As the members visit each other's homes, if they see any discrepancy in practices, they discuss the key messages learned in the GQAL sessions and the importance of practising them. In this way, an informal intra-community mechanism is maintained to support the adoption of good practices among SAMPRITI participants and non-participants (see Jahan *et al.*, 2016: 27).

Engaging youth and adolescents

Working with youth and adolescents is another important component of the current GQAL Programme. Ten young boys and girls are selected as Volunteer Youth Educators (VYEs) and invited to participate in each spot. By the end of 2015, nearly 8,000 students (4,011 boys and 3,689 girls) had participated in sessions to build capacity for anti-harassment mobilization, with their efforts reaching a total of 70,000 students directly and many more through social media. The VYEs mainly work with other young people to promote gender equality within their communities. The rationale behind this focus on youth is that it is easier for them to adopt new norms and behaviours that are supportive of gender equality. Each year, one youth gathering is arranged with all the VYEs from the programme areas. In this gathering, the VYEs share their experiences regarding gender equality with others. Another strategy to support and reinforce initiatives among the VYEs is to show docu-dramas on gender equality in local schools, with each screening followed by an open discussion. Students discuss how they can prevent gender discrimination collectively and how they can play a strong role as change-makers in their community. A 'student watch group' is also formed to address all forms of sexual harassment and to communicate with the BRAC GQAL Team.

Taking action on violence against women

Stopping VAW, an important aspect of the GQAL Programme, has been supported by a committee that aims to combat violence in all its forms. The committee members are local men and women, including religious leaders, schoolteachers and other members of the elite. In addition to acting as a monitoring body, the committee inspires individuals to take action on the basis of a Community Action Plan it has developed for addressing VAW in the locality. These efforts have been integrated with the above-mentioned school-based activities – for example, with 'community watch groups' formed in selected schools that work in collaboration with selected teachers and community leaders. This group addresses specific cases of VAW within the community and tries to resolve such problems.

The Community Leaders Forum

According to current thinking on social norms change, described in more detail in the Conclusion, we are strongly influenced by what other people do and particularly by those whom we identify as leaders. When some people adopt a specific practice in a given community or family, so the thinking goes, others eventually follow them. GQAL has therefore integrated a component into the programme that specifically engages community leaders, with the aim of encouraging them to model positive behaviours related to equitable gender norms (Jahan *et al.*, 2016: 32). The Community Leaders Forum (CLF) consists of elected local government representatives, religious leaders, teachers and other respected people who, through their influence over others in their communities, have the potential to obstruct, undermine or advance progress towards gender equality in their communities. In bimonthly CLF meetings, the members discuss how a gender-equitable or harassment-free society can be created and work accordingly to mobilize the whole community towards achieving this goal. These 'norms influencers' can and do play a critical role in shaping the emergence of positive social norms related to child marriage, women's mobility, inheritance rights and women's employment outside the home, among other issues.

Making connections

In addition to these community-level activities, GQAL engages with a range of local institutions to achieve its objectives. Interactive discussion sessions are held with various government and non-government institutions and service providers at *upazila* and union levels. The discussions aim to increase and ensure the accountability of these institutions in favour of women's rights. Gender Equality Promoters participate in these sessions and try to develop a network between service providers and themselves. In turn, service providers are invited to attend the SAMPRITI sessions so that improved access to services is available for SAMPRITI members. Once a year, a discussion meeting with *kazis* (marriage registrars) and *imams* at the union level is held to draw attention to such issues as child marriage, sexual harassment, domestic violence and women's access to economic resources. GQAL also organizes other workshops, bringing together union leadership, local elites, journalists, women leaders and representatives of other NGOs. Through these workshops and other meetings, the GQAL Programme raises awareness about the reality of discrimination and VAW in the community and works to recruit these influential actors as allies in conveying the messages of the GQAL Programme and taking action to reduce discriminatory practices.

Taken together, these various forums perform more than an (individual) awareness-raising and learning function: they 'act as a collective platform for increasing cooperation among community residents, enhancing social cohesion and ensuring intra-community responsiveness and accountability in promoting gender equality and receiving services' (Jahan *et al.*, 2016: 27). At the same time, the number and scope of the groups described above reflect the analysis underlying the GQAL methodology, namely:

> [The achievement of gender equality] needs continuous efforts, reinforcement of messages and practices from different perspectives. Not only one segment of the community, but the whole community needs to be on board and change the community members' behaviour slowly and effectively. All groups and key personnel within the community must own the key messages of GQAL to successfully follow them. These multiple forums very effectively implement this extremely important strategy.
>
> (Jahan *et al.*, 2016: 6)

Edutainment and campaigns

As noted above, prior to the relaunch of GQAL, the Gender Justice and Diversity Unit had explored the use of 'edutainment' with MEJNIN, some of the principles of which were subsequently adopted in GQAL. There were also experiments with social media campaigns in the final stages of the GQAL–CFPR–TUP collaboration. One of the innovations of the stand-alone GQAL Programme is that it has more fully adopted a quasi-campaign approach that supports the development, diffusion and uptake of key public messages related to gender equality. GQAL is designed to achieve high 'saturation' by ensuring that all the households in each selected community are covered by the multiple interventions of the programme: courtyard gatherings, FGDs, rallies, popular theatre, videos and door-to-door visits. The repetition and reinforcement of the messages via these different forums serves to amplify them.

As Jahan *et al.* (2016: 28) have noted, messages related to food, nutrition and VAW had been broadcast for some time in Bangladesh through TV talk shows and advertisements. But these did not seem to be having much impact. Through GQAL, similar messages are discussed in courtyard meetings, SAMPRITI centres and seminars – events that have helped to amplify these messages. For example, equity between men and women in nutrition and health awareness is an important aspect of GQAL's agenda. The programme relays these messages through a variety of channels, which reinforces the government advice and helps people to internalize the messages and start practising them. An important factor here is GQAL's ability to ensure that the messages are conveyed in ways that resonate directly with people's experiences, drawing on real-life stories that emerge in discussions with stakeholders. For example, on the issue of providing adequate food to pregnant women, a story of a mother-in-law choosing to feed her pregnant daughter-in-law before her husband was narrated in several GQAL sessions. Similar messages were conveyed through street theatre. The theatre troupe performed the story of an elderly woman who was knowledgeable about food and nutrition, which led to a happy and prosperous life with her husband, son, daughter-in-law and grandchildren, then constrasted this with the less happy outcomes of a character who made poor choices regarding the household distribution of food (Jahan *et al.*, 2016: 23).

Another distinctive feature of the current GQAL Programme in comparison with previous versions, which perhaps reflects its adoption of edutainment and campaigning methods, is its emphasis on developing and conveying a set of key messages on gender equality. As Jahan *et al.* (2016: 23–24) note:

> Through its long-term experience of working with BRAC staff and communities, the GQAL programme has developed relevant key messages that have been very effective in bringing transformational changes. When these messages are repeatedly shared with communities, they become part of the communities' own repertoire and gradually bring changes from within the communities.

The messages are developed in a consultative manner with key stakeholders in each community in an effort to identify the most challenging forms of gender discrimination as they are experienced in that context, and the most appropriate ways of conveying information that will help to disrupt gender roles and relations at the root of common forms of discrimination. As Jahan *et al.* (2016: 23) put it, 'the engagement of these various stakeholders builds [the] legitimacy of GQAL messages, while contextualising the key messages to fit the local realities makes them effective'. Underlying this approach is the belief that audiences are more likely to understand and welcome messages that relate to personal experience rather than those that are presented in a more abstract and less compelling way.

Thus, when working directly with women – for example, in SAMPRITI groups – or with youth educators, GQAL draws on rights-based arguments to convey ideas about women's and girls' entitlements to services or the right to enjoy a life free from violence. However, in working to shift ideas within the wider community, key messages are often conveyed 'utilising socio-economic and religious arguments' to promote the uptake of behaviours that support gender equality and the empowerment of women (Jahan *et al.*, 2016: 38). GQAL has developed a knack for strategic action in supporting different audiences to engage with gender equality. Its messages may draw, for example, on instrumental arguments related to positive economic and social returns of girls' education; or the economic benefits for the household of women's employment outside the home; or the economic, health and social benefits for the entire family of ending domestic VAW. At the same time, GQAL avoids criticizing religious viewpoints and instead attempts to utilize messages from religious teaching to support gender equality (Jahan *et al.*, 2016: 23–24).

As we have seen, the space created by GQAL initiatives using these strategies has provided women, men, boys and girls with opportunities to explore and challenge existing religious and social norms (related to the division of roles in the household, decision-making around food and other resources, women's mobility, the unacceptability of domestic violence and sexual harassment, etc.).

What were the outcomes?

The most recent GQAL Programme has invested heavily in both qualitative and quantitative studies, including quasi-experimental design, to support tracking changes over time in household gender relations. To date, it has had a positive impact in shifting participants' perceptions about women and men engaging in collective decision-making related to household purchases (land, livestock, trees and ornaments) and about who should decide when household assets are sold and how the money derived from such sales is spent (Hafiza *et al.*, 2015: 338). There is also evidence that the community GQAL Programme, like earlier work with the CFPR–TUP Programme, is contributing to changes in the division of labour at the household level, with men more likely to help with chores and childcare. Evaluation data also indicate the programme is contributing to a decrease in VAW; increased equality among girls and boys with regard to accessing nutrition, health services and education; and increased mobility for women, including taking up employment.

Evaluation reports of GQAL highlight numerous examples of SAMPRITI members feeling empowered to demand their right to access health services. One respondent, Aklima, said,

> We had several meetings with the hospital authorities. Because of that, the way the authority used to behave with us in the past if we visited the

hospital has changed. In the past, we were often asked to leave [with them] saying doctor is not present [or] there is no medicine. But now such behaviour is very rare.

(Cited in Jahan *et al.*, 2016: 19)

GQAL has also contributed to increased access to education by stressing the social and economic benefits of girls' education. For example, as reported in the research undertaken by Jahan *et al.* (2016), parents are now more likely to believe that their daughters will assist them in their old age. There are many examples of girls from GQAL communities who have found work in primary schools, the police and various NGOs. As one participant in an FGD reported:

Earlier, my husband was indifferent about our daughters' education. But his attitudes changed after watching the [TV] drama *Swapnopuron* (Realization of a Dream) by the GQAL programme. Because that drama depicted that a daughter is not a burden but an honour to the family. He has now appointed a private tutor for our daughters, got them admitted in a good quality private school. Watching him educating our daughters, many people of the community ask him: 'What is the benefit of girls' education as they will leave for others' house?' He replies, 'If the daughters can get good jobs after completing studies, then they will be able to give me all this money back. Moreover, they will treat me well when I will visit their homes.' He now believes that either son or daughter, a good child is sufficient.

(Cited in Jahan et al., 2016: 10)

The programme's activities are also having a significant impact on changing gender norms with respect to titles to land, as Nandita's story reveals.

Nandita's story

Nandita, a 30-year-old married woman from Gazipur, a town in central Bangladesh, was generally satisfied with her marriage prior to her involvement with GQAL. She reported that her husband treated her well and was never violent, while her in-laws were affluent, which provided the family with economic security. Nevertheless, she was unhappy because she had no control over the family's assets and no say in how household money was spent. Her husband believed that a woman had no need for her own money. Moreover, Nandita did all the household chores without any assistance from her husband.

Nandita recounted that the GQAL training had a dramatic effect on both herself and her husband. Her husband realized that he was treating her unfairly because he was underestimating and undermining the contribution she made to his life. After attending a number of meetings for men in his neighbourhood, he came to understand that he was discriminating against Nandita and that a happy, peaceful conjugal life depended on partnership and mutual respect. He therefore started to change his attitude and presented Nandita with a portion of land as a symbol of his respect for her and commitment to change. Nandita reported that this action filled her with a sense of dignity and confidence, as she felt that her husband had finally recognized her existence and acknowledged her contribution to the family. She also understood that women needed something of their own in order to feel confident.

(Adapted from a November 2014 interview, cited in Hafiza *et al.*, 2015: 340–341)

Efforts to analyse GQAL's role in changing attitudes attest to the complex and multi-directional nature of changes in gender relations and gender-related social norms that are associated with programmes for economic empowerment, not to mention other development interventions. For example, given some of the stories shared by programme participants,

> It is clear from GQAL that if there is an economic rationale to deviate from norms about the gender division of labour within marriage and the family, this can start a process of growing economic and gender equality within marriage, if there is support to a couple to negotiate a way through these changes.
>
> (Hafiza *et al.*, 2015: 341)

At the same time, other examples demonstrate that targeted efforts to shift attitudes about gender roles and household relations help women to access economic opportunities (see Fatema's story).

Fatema's story

Before GQAL, Fatema, a 35-year-old married woman who had studied only up to primary level, did not contribute any income to the family. She undertook unpaid household chores, while her husband worked as a share-cropper. This left the family with insufficient income. However, Fatema reported that her life changed dramatically after she and her husband participated in GQAL. Her husband no longer shouted at her; he was more caring. Fatema herself became confident and started to believe that women could accomplish anything that a man could. With her new-found confidence, she decided to start a women's cosmetics shop, and told her husband about her desire to earn her own income. Her husband assisted her in setting up the shop in the local market by seeking help from the market's secretary, who was a relative.

Fatema started her business in 2013 with a loan of 10,000 taka (US$130) and another 10,000 taka from her parents. She sourced products from both distant and local markets. As her business grew, she realized that she could double her profits if she could find a way to sell her goods in Dhaka, which was nearly 100 kilometres from her home. Initially, her husband accompanied her on her trips to the capital, but now she goes alone.

Fatema faced many challenges establishing a business amid 150 other shops that were run by men. Moreover, people gossiped about her and tried to influence her husband. However, Fatema reported that she did not care about their opinions. Her husband now consults her and asks for advice, and he sometimes helps with the shopkeeping. Other women also come to her for advice about starting their own businesses.

(Adapted from a November 2014 interview, cited in Hafiza *et al.*, 2015: 342)

The current GQAL phase is informed by an awareness that changing gender relations within the family is inadequate unless wider society and state services come forward in support of such changes. As we have seen, GQAL supports community-based collective action to ensure women's access to different state and non-state services.

Kolpona's story

Kolpona Rani Sarker is a GQAL-led SAMPRITI member at Ramrail village in the eastern district of Brahmanbaria. As a SAMPRITI member, she bargains with Union Parishad (UP), the lowest tier of local government, to gain access to various services. She has also learned about gender-based rights, discrimination, VAW and so on. One day, along with other SAMPRITI members, she visited Ramrail's Union Parishad to request training on the operation of sewing machines and obtain some guidance on production. After the meeting, she attended a 15-day training course, which enabled her to engage in income-generating activities.

(Adapted from an October 2014 interview, cited in Hafiza et al., 2015: 343)

This phase of GQAL has continued to clarify the relationship between gender equality and economic empowerment for BRAC (see Hafiza *et al.*, 2015 for a full discussion). While BRAC has contributed significantly to poverty reduction and women's economic empowerment since the 1980s, over time it has become increasingly evident that women's self-employment on its own does not necessarily pull vast numbers of women out of poverty (whether we understand women's poverty in relation to intra-household poverty or in relation to household income levels, which are the focus of current concerns about growing inequality in society). A focus on self-employment alone, as we have seen, did not result in challenges to the patriarchal structures of inequality. However, programmes like GQAL, which take a gender-equality approach to poverty alleviation, are employing a gender analysis of poverty and the linkages between gender inequality and economic inequality, and these are succeeding. In the GQAL experience, including the examples provided above, we can see that addressing gender equality within households can be an essential step to women's economic empowerment, rather than vice versa. Attitudinal change among women and men can lead to changes in gender roles, including women taking up self-employment (Hafiza *et al.*, 2015: 344).

Changing lives in one generation

In 1999, when the Gender Team was designing GQAL for VOs, it chaired FGDs in half a dozen peri-urban and rural communities in Bangladesh. Typically, these meetings would consist of about 20 women who were clients of various BRAC programmes, especially the Micro-finance Programme. Clustered around the seated women were children and curious men onlookers. At that time, it was very difficult for the women to imagine a future for their daughters that would be any different from their own lives. Try as we might to stimulate discussion through stories and examples, the women lacked the confidence to speak up, and they were unable to look beyond their current existence.

By 2015, a dramatic change had taken place. Groups of BRAC women clients – from the oldest to the youngest – told stories of how their lives were changing and how they were exercising their rights and fighting for the extension of those rights to others in their communities. Mothers spoke about the role of education in allowing their daughters to succeed as teachers, doctors or lawyers. Boys talked about combating the sexual harassment of their sisters and female friends by discussing the harmful effects of 'eve-teasing' with their male classmates. Their stories gave life and meaning to the hard statistical evidence on the changes in gender relations that Bangladesh is currently experiencing (see Table 1.1 in Chapter 1).

In total, since 2001, the GQAL Programme has reached over 2 million village women and men through courtyard meetings and other direct actions. In these village communities, tens of thousands of women and men, girls and boys, have participated in GQAL sessions and then shared what they learned with their friends and neighbours. From the outset, the programme was countercultural in the sense that power relations were addressed upfront in the design stage. GQAL in the community helped to highlight the importance of changing gender relations at the household and community levels, including working with men as well as women as agents of change for gender equality and creating spaces for both men and women to negotiate these complex and at times confusing changes.

Here we can see most vividly the thread that runs through GQAL in all its versions. By creating safe and supportive spaces over the past two decades, GQAL has helped women and men to articulate their experiences and feelings in ways that would have been very challenging within their own families and communities. Socializing the experience meant that both women and men were able to understand that another way of living was possible – one that necessitated changing discriminatory gender norms and practices. It also allowed them to identify the small (and large) steps they needed to take in order to make that change a reality.

Notes

1　Personal communication from Sheepa Hafiza, former Director of GJD, 26 November 2016.
2　As we have attempted to show in previous chapters, GQAL is based on different principles from standard 'training'. We began by calling the sessions with community members 'GQAL orientations', but 'training' gradually became the term that was most often used by staff, managers and evaluators. We also started with the term 'GQAL facilitator' rather than 'GQAL trainer', but again staff defaulted to the latter term.
3　See, for example, the findings of Schuler *et al.* (1999: 123), which highlight the mixture and complexity of outcomes for women participating in micro-finance programmes. On the one hand, credit may reduce domestic violence by increasing family resources and allowing women to organize into solidarity groups that help to publicize gender inequality and the problem of violence; on the other, providing resources to women and encouraging them to maintain control over those resources may provoke male violence, as men feel their authority is undermined. See also Goetz and Sen Gupta (1996).
4　This section draws largely on unpublished evaluation reports, specifically Mahmud and Mahbub (2004), as well as interviews with BRAC staff.
5　Control groups were defined as communities in which BRAC had a presence through progammes other than GQAL (e.g., Credit, Health, Education, etc.), or where there were community meetings related to BRAC issues, but no programmes. Programme groups were those in which the only BRAC intervention was GQAL.
6　An *upazila* is a sub-unit of a district; it is the second-lowest tier of regional administration in Bangladesh.
7　Personal communication from Sheepa Hafiza, former Director of GJD, 26 November 2016.
8　Although the programme's designers had always intended to include an element of community theatre, this initiative did not get off the ground in GQAL–CFPR–TUP as it was beyond the capacity of the team to develop appropriate gender-sensitive scenes and there were insufficient resources to implement the plan.
9　CFPR–TUP used the term 'spots' to identify programme intervention areas, as the ultra poor often live in very scattered areas. We have elected to use the term 'areas' in this book.
10　This information was shared by M. Kairy, BRAC's Chief Financial Officer at the time.
11　Educational entertainment – 'edutainment' – is designed to educate as well as inform or amuse. The following explanation comes from the UN Virtual Knowledge Centre to End Violence Against Women and Girls: 'TV and radio serial dramas ("soap operas") are the best-known contemporary forms of edutainment. They appeal to their viewers' minds and emotions, developing multi-layered storylines inspired by people's daily lives over successive installments. Their characters offer

opportunities for emotional identification and role modeling. Popular series maintain long-term contact with their viewers, exposing them to different aspects of the same theme over several months or years.' For more information, see www.endvawnow.org/en/articles/1268-educational-entertainment-edutainment.html.

12 This terms refers to the Gender Justice Educators, the Volunteer Youth Educators and the SAMPRITI members.

13 This discussion of GQAL components and stakeholders draws heavily on Jahan *et al.* (2016).

References

Alim, A. (2007) *Changes in Knowledge, Perception, and Attitudes of the Villagers towards Gender Roles and Gender Relations: An Evaluation of Gender Quality Action Learning Programme*, BRAC Research Report, Dhaka: BRAC Research and Evaluation Division.

BRAC (2013) 'MEJNIN: Safe Citizenship for Girls', fact sheet, Dhaka: BRAC.

Das, N., Yasmin, R., Ara, J., Kamruzzaman, Md., Davis, P., Quisumbing, A., Roy, S. (2013) 'How Do Intrahousehold Dynamics Change when Assets Are Transferred to Women? Evidence from BRAC's "Targeting the Ultra Poor" Programme in Bangladesh', Gender and Agriculture and Assets Project (GAAP) note, Rome: International Food Policy Research Institute.

Gender Justice and Diversity, BRAC (2014) 'MEJNIN Monitoring Report', unpublished report, Dhaka: BRAC.

Ghuznavi, F. (2008) *From Action-Learning, to Learning to Act: Lessons from GQAL*, Dhaka: Gender Justice and Diversity Section, BRAC.

Goetz, A.-M., Sen Gupta, R. (1996) 'Who Takes the Credit? Gender, Power, and Control over Loan Use in Rural Credit Programmes in Bangladesh', *World Development*, 24.1: 45–63.

Hafiza, S., Kamruzzaman, M., Begum, A.H. (2015) 'Addressing Multiple Dimensions of Gender Inequality: The Experience of the BRAC Gender Quality Action Learning (GQAL) Programme in Bangladesh', *Gender and Development*, 23.2: 333–346.

Jahan, F., Shahan, A.M., Reza Khan, S., Akter-uz-zaman, S., Jahan, M. with assistance from Karim, R. (2016) 'Gender Quality Action and Learning Programme: Documenting the "Transformations Achieved" and the "Process of Achieving Them"', unpublished report, Dhaka: Gender Justice and Diversity Division, BRAC.

Mahmud, S., Mahbub, A. (2004) 'Report on the Evaluation of the Pilot Project on GQAL Programme with BRAC VO', unpublished evaluation report, Dhaka: BRAC.

Mahmud, S., Sultan, M., Huq, L. (2012) *Assessing the Performance of GQAL in Changing Gender Norms and Behaviour*, Dhaka: BRAC Development Institute.

Schuler, S.R., Hashemi, S.M., Badal, S.H. (1999) 'Men's Violence against Women in Rural Bangladesh: Undermined or Exacerbated by Microcredit Programmes?' in D. Eade (ed.), *Development with Women: Selected Essays from Development in Practice*, Oxford: Oxfam GB.

RED (2013) *MEJNIN Pilot (2010–2011) Evaluation Report*, RED Working Paper No. 39, Dhaka: BRAC.

5 Conclusion

As a result of our work with GQAL, we have been given an opportunity to reflect a great deal on how change happens. In this chapter, we begin with an overview of the outcomes achieved through GQAL and then offer our assessment of critical factors that contributed to these outcomes. We then turn to current literature and debates pertinent to the GQAL story – for example, on gender mainstreaming, organizational change, New Institutionalism and gender-sensitive evaluation – providing an overview of how thinking has shifted since 1994, when we first started working with BRAC to support gender-equality change. We end the chapter with our observations on what GQAL contributes to theory and practice (which may be of interest to other organizations) and its limitations (what we might have done differently, given what we know now). Lastly, we share our overall conclusions about the impact of GQAL.

The first conclusion of this remarkable story is that change is possible.[1] Maxine Molyneux famously described gender equality as requiring not only a change in a woman's *condition* – whether she had enough to eat and a roof over her head – but also in her *position* – her ability to make choices and have a say about her life (Molyneux, 2010). Previous chapters have documented a range of changes of both kinds within BRAC and in the communities where BRAC works. These changes notably include a variety of examples of changed power relations both within BRAC and in the communities where GQAL was implemented. Figure 5.1 summarizes these changes.[2]

The figure illustrates changes in both the staff and the community GQAL. The top-left quadrant shows changes related to attitudes, values and behaviours. We see that, inside BRAC, staff increased respect for women and their role in society. This translated into better working relationships and increased decision-making for BRAC women staff. In the community, we see changed understandings of women's role in the household and attitudinal changes on the part of women and men with regard to sharing household chores. Encouragingly, it also seems that the programme began to change attitudes in response to domestic violence.

Looking at the top-right quandrant, we see an increase in the resources available to women. Inside BRAC, there was an increase in the retention of women staff (although that later ebbed away). In the community, women had

Consciousness and Capabilities

- Changes to women's and men's attitudes regarding gender relations inside BRAC and in communities

- Better working relationships and problem-solving inside BRAC

- Awareness and mobilization against domestic violence

Access to Resources and Opportunities

- Some increase in number of women staff in BRAC

- Increase in women's control of assets

- Increased women's access to healthcare and nutrition

Social Norms and Deep Structures

- Changed perception of women's role in the household

- Increase in women's decision-making

- Men doing household chores

- Inside BRAC: increased appreciation of women's contribution and role in society

Formal Rules, Policies and Accountability Mechanisms

- Internal policies such as gender policy, parental leave, transport, sexual harassment

- Influence on government policies locally and nationally

- New programmes such as MEJNIN and SAMPRITI

- Process for dealing with sexual harassment within BRAC

Figure 5.1 GQAL outcomes

more control over assets as well as greater access to health and nutrition services (Jahan *et al.*, 2016; Mahmud *et al.*, 2012)

In the bottom-right quadrant, we see the development of new policies and programmes. Inside BRAC, these comprise a variety of gender-sensitive policies, including the development of a gender policy and its update, the institution of a sexual harassment policy and process, and the implementation of a host of new programmes in support of gender equality, such as SAMPRITI, MEJNIN and others.

In the bottom-left quandrant, we see the evolution of norms and the effects on the deep structure of BRAC and the culture of Bangladeshi communities. Inside BRAC, in the Area Offices, we see increased appreciation of women's contributions and a concomitant increase in respect for women as colleagues. In the community, we see challenges to patriarchal norms regarding decision-making, food sharing and household chores, and to the tacit acceptance of domestic violence.

Also depicted in Figure 5.1 is the evolution of work on gender equality within BRAC. The bulk of programming BRAC offered to women in 1994 was concentrated in the upper-right quadrant of the Framework – skills training, micro-credit, health services and education. If there was investment in the left-hand side – consciousness of and support for gender equality – it was usually directed towards individuals. GQAL was special, in both staff and community versions, because it deliberately targeted the lower-left as well as the upper-left quadrant. The programme explored what was invisible in culture and used that knowledge to transform gender-related norms. It is in shifting these norms, which often inhibit change in resource allocation and behaviour, that we can make greater equality a reality. GQAL is one of very few large-scale organizational-change and gender-equality-change initiatives to focus on the lower-left quadrant.

It is also interesting to note that both MEJNIN and the more recent stand-alone GQAL Programme focus on the lower-right quadrant, which represents the government policies and initiatives that support an enabling environment for gender equality. Over the years, GJD staff have lobbied the government over gender-equality policies and programmes; this is now being carried into the GQAL community programmes to engage citizens in advocacy.

Factors that contributed to GQAL's success

The programme was made possible through the sponsorship of BRAC's Executive Director and later Chair of the Governing Board, F.H. Abed. Also, the participatory process of diagnosis and developing GQAL ensured that BRAC managers and the GQAL Team 'owned' the initiative and had adequate time to reach a consensus about how to approach it. This included long discussions about contending understandings and possibilities.

If these two factors made GQAL possible, the first key factor which made the staff GQAL successful was the commitment of GQAL trainers and the willingness of BRAC staff and managers to open themselves to quite challenging ideas. In order to understand this willingness, we will look at three key dimensions: context, power and individual–collective learning.

Context

Although BRAC prided itself on being a social pioneer, it was still nested in a patriarchal society. Also, BRAC (like any large organization) was and is not a monolith; when the decision was taken to improve gender relations, it was not the case that anyone who disagreed was considered out of step. On the contrary, the BRAC community comprised a wide range of opinions about how important it was to work on gender equality. Some people thought it was fundamentally wrong; others felt that, while women's empowerment might be a good thing, it was less important than more pressing matters; and a third group supported the idea of empowerment but were not prepared to accept ancillary changes, such as fast-tracking women managers. Finally, there were those who, for various reasons, were fully committed to gender-equitable change. This pluralism meant that we could not imagine a perfect universe and train people towards it via policies and accountability systems alone. Instead, we listened, debated and developed understandings of gender at BRAC that would provide a starting point for learning. The programme's win–win approach to conflict negotiation and its marriage of gender equality with programme quality were very appealing to both staff and managers. In particular, the idea of problem-solving that would provide an alternative to 'shifting blame' was very important to senior managers.

From the start, the GQAL Team was committed to engaging staff – in meaningful and non-judgemental ways – in defining what gender equality meant and how it would be practised day to day within BRAC. In the course of these discussions, the team tried to balance its own understandings of gender equality with a pragmatic understanding of what would work in BRAC's organizational culture. As Rieky Stuart said at the time, 'There are no perfect places to start, only real ones.' This context-driven pragmatism, coupled with a dedication to achieving substantive and sustained progress on goals related to gender equality, has characterized the programme throughout its run.

Power

In the GQAL Programme (at both staff and community level), change required the formal approval of senior management; that green light was, however, far from enough. Also essential was a space that allowed people to analyse their social situation from a gendered point of view, feel the support of a sympathetic collective, exert agency for change, and see those new behaviours become norms and, in some cases, formal policies.

Traditional understandings of power in organizations rely on clear rules and a set of rewards and punishments to enforce behaviour. Given the context described above, this was an unlikely path for us to take. We needed to utilize other types of power. We knew that, for generations, women and men had worked with visible and invisible circuits of power to challenge inequality (VeneKlasen and Miller, 2002).

In looking back at our experience, we are struck by the importance of 'agency' – that is, the agency to resist, challenge, disrupt existing norms and transform ways of living and working. It is the power to speak and act for oneself in one's organization and one's community. This power of agency may be expressed publicly through petitions, demonstrations or marches, or it may be expressed more privately in personal relations with spouses and families. For some, agency may arise from a more self-generated sense of worth and a capacity to learn through experimentation (Kegan and Lahey, 2009); much of the literature on transformative change (e.g., Taylor, 2011), however, emphasizes the importance of social support.

In the case of GQAL, agency was supported by:

- relationship: the power of acceptance and compassion that supports the personal risks that attend learning and change;
- the collective: the energy that comes from solidarity, from struggling with others in a just cause;
- imagination: the ability to imagine a new world; and
- critical analysis and local knowledge: the power to understand, to strategize and to act with clarity of purpose.[3]

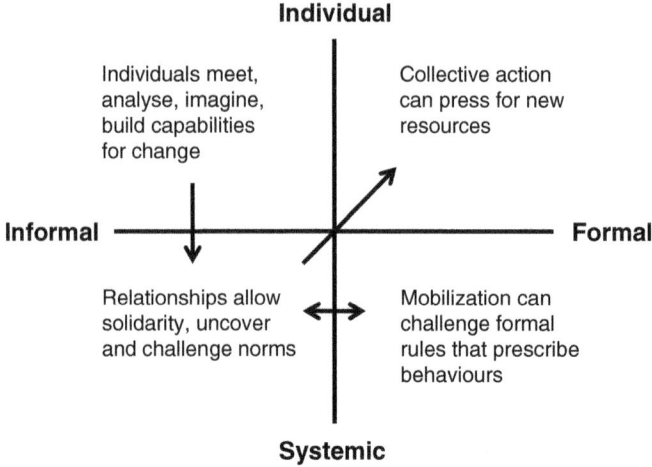

Figure 5.2 Pathways to power
Note: Arrows are illustrative; many other pathways are possible.

Figure 5.2 illustrates how these different types of power can be used to shift norms of inequality. Analysis brings new information and allows us to imagine and recalibrate norms and escape from preformed understandings. Relationship allows for collectivity and the capacity to challenge social norms and mobilize for change. Mobilization can demand change in the formal rules and the pre-scriptions of behaviour. This, in turn, contributes to the challenging of social norms and facilitates further changes in consciousness (Rao *et al.*, 2016: 33).

Another aspect of power in the GQAL Programme was the power we held as consultants and staff of BRAC. We were asked to improve gender relations within the organization. However, as we have discussed above, 'gender' was a very fluid and contested idea that needed to be defined. The GQAL Team had the power of knowledge and relationship in that discussion, but our power was conditioned by the context in which we found ourselves. We wanted to push certain ideas about gender equality that we held, but at the same time we knew those ideas needed to find broad acceptance within the pluralistic context of BRAC. In other words, we needed to remain true to the 'one leg' theory,[4] while simultaneously creating the conditions for more fundamental changes in power relations. We were not directly advocating for deeper change. Rather, we created spaces where participants would see the need for change, generate support for it, then act.

Not everyone agrees with this approach to using power for change. For example, Sohela Nazneen (2007), in her thoughtful study of BRAC and Proshika, argues that these changes require accountability structures, and if the programme has not challenged the primacy of loan targets, then those loan targets will remain the priority accountability measure. Gender issues will always be subsidiary. This argument echoes the one that human rights should trump all other government decisions. This is as unlikely as gender equality becoming the dominant value in an organization like BRAC. We believe, like Ignatieff and Guttman (2003), that human rights are an important consideration in government policy-making, though not necessarily the primary one. Similarly, an organization such as BRAC has many purposes, including delivering services (as gender equitably as possible) to large numbers of people. It would be an interesting debate as to whether BRAC's members would be better served if gender-outcome indicators were the primary measures of success, but that discussion was not on the table and it is not particularly useful today. The more important question for BRAC is whether its other measures of success could be efficiently and effectively achieved *without* paying attention to gender equality, and, if not, whether consistently including gender-related outcomes in its organizational strategy and programme design and outreach would improve its overall performance as a dispenser of credit and services to the rural poor. The GQAL evaluation of the GQAL–CFPR–TUP collaboration shows, for example, that overall performance improves, and there are positive gender-equality results, when gendered power dynamics are taken into account.

Individual–collective learning

Translating the learning of individuals into organizational change has been a key dilemma of organizational studies for decades. When organizational development was invented in the 1960s, it was precisely in response to management training programmes that were not leading to changed organizations (Beckhard, 1969). Research some 15 years later showed that learning beyond knowledge and attitudinal change occurred only later, on the job, and that this learning was dependent on systemic factors (Kelleher *et al.*, 1986). More recent work (Beer *et al.*, 2016) demonstrates that this dilemma is alive and well in corporate America. Beer and colleagues' research on the organizational impact of training found that a very small proportion of training efforts result in change. They tell the story of an organization that invested heavily in a training programme for all employees:

Participants described the program as very powerful. For a whole week, they engaged in numerous tasks that required teamwork, and they received real-time feedback on both individual and group behavior. The program ended with a plan for taking the learning back into the organization. Pre- and post-training surveys suggested that participants' attitudes had changed.

A couple of years later, when a new general manager came in to lead the division, he requested an assessment of the costly program. As it turned out, managers thought little had changed as a result of the training, even though it had been inspiring at the time. They found it impossible to apply what they had learned about teamwork and collaboration, because of a number of managerial and organizational barriers. '[The previous GM] had a significant impact on our organization, with all of us reflecting him in our managerial style,' a member of the division's senior team explained during an interview. 'We are all more authoritarian than before.'

(Beer *et al.*, 2016: 1)

A recent review of gender training programmes found that although gender training had proliferated since the Beijing Platform for Action in 1995, there was little information on its impact (UN Women, 2015). The review found that training seldom altered the structural and power relations that perpetuate inequality. The participants in the Bergen Conference on Gender Training (Rao *et al.*, 1991) also understood that training was not enough; that concerted efforts at organizational change were also required.

GQAL dealt with this dilemma of promoting individual learning and facilitating systemic change in five key ways:

1   Strong endorsement from BRAC's leader. The Executive Director was a strong sponsor of the programme and was respected by the staff. His investment in the programme gave its messages greater institutional relevance; he also modelled behaviour with which staff could identify.
2   Learning in teams. Participants were not sent individually to training programmes. They learned together, as teams.
3   Safe spaces for personal reflection and social transformation. GQAL created a space for participants to reflect on their collective experience. The programme treated participants not as individuals to be 'trained', but as individuals who were collectively examining their own beliefs, behaviour and social setting with a view to improving their lives, their work culture and their society.
4   Collective and reflexive action. Participants took collective action and evaluated that action in order to continue the change process.
5   Local-to-global learning. Issues beyond the capacity of Area Offices were brought to the attention of regional and senior managers, who in many cases were able to translate local problem-solving into organizational learning.

These key practices mirror what was found to be important by Beer et al. (2016) in their study of leadership training and organizational change in private-sector organizations. The authors highlight the importance of top management articulating the direction of change, supporting bottom-up analysis of problems, facilitating day-to-day coaching and consultation, developing new metrics of evaluation,[5] and adjusting the reward structure accordingly. Of particular importance to us is the need for an ongoing process of learning. Just as organizations do not do accounting or sales for six months and then move on to something else, learning and change for gender equality is an ongoing task.

Community GQAL

GQAL in the community has become BRAC's primary means of working with key stakeholders to address gender-equality issues. Its success can be traced to many of the same factors that were embedded in the staff GQAL. For example, involving women and men as change agents in the community was very effective; the creation of space for women's and men's agency to act against gender injustice has been a notable feature. This approach has also been adopted by a number of organizations, in part in response to growing awareness of the under-conceptualization of the role of men and boys in 'gender' equality and, related to this, the understanding that spaces and processes for engaging both women *and* men are needed (Reemer, 2015; Jewkes *et al.*, 2014). Using this approach does not exclude same-sex meetings, but because the overall intention of the programme is to engage women and men in creating greater equality, and it consciously frames equality as being in the self-interest of both sexes, the tone that is fostered is one of problem-solving, rather than blame.

We believe the following factors, discussed in the previous chapter, were critical to the effectiveness of the community GQAL Programme:

• The use of skilled trainers who were able to craft safe spaces for sometimes very heated discussions between women and men. These trainers were able to frame gender issues as social issues for which we were seeking solutions. BRAC consciously invested in the training of trainers through regular Capacity Development Forums.

• As in the staff GQAL, participants were involved in an analysis of their lived experience. Women participants commented on how they appreciated the sessions because they related to 'real life'.

• The programme went far beyond training individuals. It included men and families, and also reached out to the broader community, engaging with religious leaders, politicians, journalists, government officials and other members of the elite. The connection with neighbourhood and school committees created an enabling environment for the creation of new local norms.

• The programme (and its facilitators) were also able to intervene on an emergency basis in the case of violence or threatened early marriage.

Beyond these factors lay the transformative potential of imagination. Sheepa Hafiza, former Director of the GJD Unit, believes that women and men embraced these changes once they understood that a different way of living was possible:

> Gender-sensitive changes happened in women's and men's lives in a very short period once they realized that a different, respectful, loving and peaceful life is possible. I believe that these women and men had been groomed with a very strong stereotyped pessimistic notion that men should be rude, arrogant, decisive as a 'man', bound to exercise power by demeaning or beating women and children as a ritual. That was called masculinity. [They believed], without that, a man was nothing (with no respect or trust) in the society. On the other hand, women are valued as submissive, helpful, quiet, shy, hidden, stupid and hard workers [who get by] without recognition.

GQAL discussion orientation and the role-plays challenged those ideologies and showed them another life is possible, where they can be friends, partners and dependent on each other, which brings benefits for them and the society that are visible, even tangible – once realized – BINGO, they are different people.[6]

To the authors' knowledge, the research on GQAL in the community is one of the first large-scale and rigorous evaluations of work undertaken to change cultural norms. The evidence indicates that there was both attitudinal and behavioural change, and that the implementation of this change initiative in tandem with programmes that offered resources, services and skills led to better results in both areas.

Current literature and GQAL

In order to locate the GQAL story within the current literature, we reviewed recent and relevant work related to gender mainstreaming, New Institutionalism, normative and organizational change and gender-sensitive programme and impact evaluation. For example, recent work by the Gender and Development Network (GADN) and UN Women indicates an emerging consensus regarding best approaches to gender mainstreaming. A recent briefing by the GADN (Derbyshire *et al.*, 2015) proposed a comprehensive framework that identifies the importance of an enabling environment and internal and external gender-equality champions, whose commitment and energy are converted into gender analyses, gender-disaggregated data and gender-sensitive programme design and evaluation; the combination of these actors and processes leads to interventions that advance gender equality.

The GADN framework (Derbyshire *et al.*, 2015) offers a map of important factors that are likely to contribute to successful outcomes. Unlike many other frameworks, it addresses the importance of an organization as an enabling environment. But its conceptualization of that enabling environment emphasizes senior management, technical gender staff and clear success strategies predicated on awareness-raising by gender focal points and external pressure from women's groups and donors. These are all important drivers of change, but we believe that the framework underestimates the difficulty and importance of changing the attitudes and values of the actors involved, as well the cultural and institutional world(s) they inhabit.

Similarly, a very comprehensive report from a UN Women Expert Group (Cohen *et al.*, 2013) recommends four ways forward:

- Strategic planning to design and adopt gender mainstreaming at the country level; multiple-track approaches and integrating gender into core national development strategies, such as macro-economic policy.
- Matching the programme cycle, which involves undertaking gender assessments and gender-sensitive programme analysis, prioritizing interventions, engaging in results formulation and so on.

- Mixing gender and context analysis and planning tools, including gender-based budgeting, to become more strategic.
- Improving the integration of gender results in results based management (RBM) frameworks.

Taken together, these are described as elements of 'a strategic approach' to gender mainstreaming as part of the post-2015 development framework. The report is a very strong guideline in many respects, but apart from referencing a draft version of the GADN framework as an organizational change theory, it is also silent on the personal and institutional transformations that are required to implement these ideas.

Our concern about the lack of attention that is paid to personal and institutional change does not stem merely from personal experience. The New Institutional (NI) literature has been very helpful in explaining how 'institutions' shape actors' behaviour either to advance or resist change. The term 'institutions' refers to the collection of formal and informal norms and rules that constitute our shared understanding of 'how the world works' (Mackay *et al.*, 2010). NI writers have described how this goes beyond explicit rules to include symbol systems, cognitive scripts and moral templates. Alvesson and Billing (2009), in describing gender dynamics in organizations, identify three levels of the system that constrain change: institutions, interaction and identities. They argue, and we agree, that a change process requires attention to all three.

Mukhopadhyay and her colleagues ask us to step back from the processes of change to look at what they call the 'govermentalities' at play, and at how organizations take in feminist principles and then alter them to fit existing understandings of power, the dominant norms of the organization and development itself (Mukhopadhyay and Wong, 2007; Milward *et al.*, 2015). Rosalind Eyben describes how 'power, working invisibly, [makes] us concur with inappropriate methods for designing and assessing programmes with multiple pathways of change' (quoted in Milward *et al.*, 2015: 79), the implications of which we explore below.

Another big shift since 1994 is the current focus on 'social norms' in development discourse, which signals greater awareness that interventions failing to address gender-related social norms may have limited impact on women's and girls' choices and chances. There is also an increased interest in understanding how gender norms change, with recent research drawing attention to the effects of economic incentives, broad social changes such as urbanization and demographic change, education, access to new ideas through the media, role models, legal change and policies and programmes that promote gender-norm change and social mobilization and campaigning (ODI, 2014; World Bank, 2011, 2014).

Looking more broadly at organizational studies and norms, it is arguable that organizational theorists have known that norms trump management leadership and incentives as far back as the Western Electric studies undertaken by Mayo and Roethlisberger in the 1920s.[7] Work on organizational development beginning in the 1960s (Beckhard, 1969) and organizational culture in the 1980s (Cameron and Quinn, 2006; Schein, 2004) led to a broad understanding that cultural issues shape and constrain what is possible in organizational change. At some point, a wise, if weary, change-maker coined the now much-quoted organizational truism that 'culture eats strategy for breakfast'.

These understandings of the importance of personal and socio-cultural factors have led to a series of sophisticated conceptions of how change happens at a cultural level in organizations. All of them work with the deeper dynamics of personal learning, team relations and organizational design. All demand long-term, ongoing efforts (Scharmer, 2009; Weisbord, 2012; Kegan and Lahey, 2009).

In our own work on 'deep structures', we have documented how taken-for-granted (and therefore invisible) assumptions about how organizations work are deeply patriarchal and also resist change in a variety of ways. In a recent book (Rao *et al.*, 2016: 145), we described how difficult it is to shift deep structures as a result of five characteristics:

- *They are often invisible, so 'normal' and taken for granted by organizational insiders that they are unquestioned.* For example, in many organizations, working long hours is viewed as a sign of commitment and is often necessary for promotion. However, this unstated requirement has a differential effect on women who have a disproportionate responsibility for home and childcare.
- *They are layered and mutually reinforcing.* Chipping away at one layer of embedded discrimination can simply lead to revealing another layer. Another aspect of deep structure that reinforces this norm is the high value accorded to instrumentality – work above all else. All these aspects intertwine to form a web that is difficult to pull apart and change.
- *They are constantly being reproduced.* In every conversation, every process, every decision, power works in a way to produce and reproduce discriminatory norms and structure unequal gender power relations. This is what Mackay (2011) calls the 'daily enactment of institutions'. This dynamism shows how discriminatory social norms and deep structure are normalized within organizations and also points to how new formulations, new alliances and new practices can be deliberately inserted into daily discourse to destabilize them.
- *They are highly resilient and often come back in new forms to quash what seemed like a victory.* Decades of work on spotlighting gender discriminatory policies and practices in organizations has led to a broad awareness of inequities such as pay differentials, sexual harassment, family–work balance issues and implementation of compensatory policies such as equal pay, and fast tracking women in management. However, in new spaces of engagement that have opened up, such as cyberspace, the rules have to be negotiated all over again.
- *They are both unchanging and can change.* Gender power hierarchies are the 'sticky stuff' (World Bank, 2011) that constrain gender equality everywhere in the world. Yet, Gender at Work's experience working with over

100 organizations in the last 15 years has taught us that social norms and deep structure in organizations can change.

Taken together, the work on institutions, organizations and deep structures points to the importance of both personal change and change in the normative structure of an organization if that organization is going to be capable of changing the barriers in its systems and work practices to advance a gender-equality agenda that is concerned with altering the power relations between women and men. This is why the staff GQAL story is so interesting. It is a large-scale, documented effort to alter internal organizational norms and design new ways of working in response to those new norms.

Recent work on 'adaptive development' adds to our understanding of how to make changes of this magnitude. As we mentioned in the Introduction, adaptive development promotes four principles (O'Neil, 2016: 9):

- Support change led by local stakeholders, not external funders.
- Start with problems or issues, not ready-made solutions.
- Be politically informed and use smart tactics.
- Build learning and adaptation into organizations and programmes.

Of particular interest with respect to the GQAL story is the importance of starting with problems as opposed to ready-made solutions. Particularly in the staff GQAL, teams were supported in analysing their context and developing definitions of problems; they then went on to develop solutions that made sense to them. O'Neil makes the point that gender norms are context-specific and the environment in which the change is implemented may have many moving parts. The analysis needs to look at underlying causes, not just symptoms, but as O'Neil (2016: 11) reminds us, 'implementers' imperfect analysis is better than more polished studies undertaken by external consultants'.

Also important to GQAL is the injunction to be politically smart. We interpret that, in the GQAL case, as being politically savvy and understanding the need for solutions that meet the needs of different constituencies. When we began the staff GQAL, we worked for nine months on the needs assessment and negotiating a programme design before we actually launched the pilot. This meant that the programme was able to gain acceptance from a wide range of managers. The programme that emerged was not everything we wanted, but it was a very strong beginning.

Measuring gender-equality change

One of the threads running through this book is the increased importance that has been attached over time to demonstrating GQAL results and ensuring the results are achieved in a cost-effective manner. These concerns mirror the rise of the 'results' and 'evidence' agendas in international development over the past two decades, though, as noted in the Introduction, the results-driven culture (e.g., loan repayment rates) was a key feature of BRAC's micro-finance work even in 1994. This section reviews the wider literature on measurement and reflects on what GQAL contributes to current debates. Three specific trends that have emerged since 1994 are reviewed here, to the extent that they impact on gender-equality work: the influence of experimental design to evaluate programme 'success'; the monetization of the 'value' of programme outcomes, especially the emphasis on cost-effectiveness and 'value for money'; and efforts to widen how 'success' and 'value' are defined and assessed as a way of ensuring that decisions about how money is spent take into consideration both social justice and efficiency concerns.

In response to demands for rigorously derived evidence of results, rando-mized control trials (RCTs) and quasi-experimental techniques have come to prominence in the evaluation of development programmes. These methods depend on the random selection of programme participants into 'treatment' and 'control' groups, and the collection of panel data to determine the impact of an intervention. The aim is to investigate whether there is evidence to show a causal link between the programme intervention and outcome-level change. The approach is seen as the 'gold standard' in impact evaluation and holds sig-nificant influence over judgements on 'what works', what interventions are deemed 'successful' and, in turn, what types of programmes and interventions should receive funding (Smith *et al.*, 2011). As we have seen throughout the story of GQAL in the community, such methods have been increasingly used at BRAC to demonstrate programme impact.

The related discussion of 'value for money' and how to assess it has also emerged as a touchstone over the last ten years. The meaning of 'value for money' is a matter of debate, though essentially it provides a framework to assess the economy, efficiency and effectiveness of the design of a programme or activity. Cost–benefit analysis is one commonly used tool to assess whether an intervention's monetized benefits (i.e., expected outcomes) outweigh its costs.

'Value for money' assessments are being used to assess whether gender-equality outcomes are being achieved in a cost-effective and efficient manner. For some, this approach is considered pragmatic and strategic, given that in the current context of funding scarcity it is wise to 'prove' the effectiveness of programme interventions in order to secure or maintain funding for gender equality and women's rights. As we observed in Chapter 4, the analysis of the costs of GQAL–CFPR–TUP relative to the overall CFPR–TUP Programme costs (4 per cent) suggests that, for a very small investment, efforts to main-stream gender into BRAC programmes can have positive benefits in terms of gender-equality outcomes (economic assets and resources and changes in atti-tudes, behaviour and social norms in families and communities) as well as improving efficiency in programme implementation and the achievement of other (non-gender-related) programme outcomes.

The preoccupation with 'evidence' and 'value for money' is also contributing in positive ways to clarifying thinking about how gender-equality outcomes are conceptualized and how these can be effectively measured (or not). For example, it has challenged thinking about how to evaluate investments in gender mainstreaming and related organizational-change efforts. Critics have observed that organizations that have applied gender-mainstreaming strategies and attempted to address ways in which their organizations reproduce gender inequalities have failed to assess how these internal processes have contributed to programme outcomes (Brouwers, 2013 and Watkins, 2004, both cited in Milward *et al.*, 2015: 77–78). A recent system-wide review of UN efforts to advance gender equality and women's empowerment goes further, calling for a shift from focusing solely on gender-mainstreaming processes to simultaneous examination of the results of those processes. The current gap is seen to relate partly to poorly articulated theories of change – and the insufficient testing of those theories – about how gender-mainstreaming structures and processes contribute to gender equality results and to development results in general (UN Women, 2015). Currently, the 'link between the structures and processes and their results is weak or missing' (UN Women, 2015: 13).

In this book, we have attempted to respond to this concern by demonstrating the linkages between the new problem-solving skills and gender knowledge of staff who participated in GQAL and their improved performance as regards working with members of BRAC communities to promote gender equality. Specifically, the modelling of new social norms surrounding women's work and mobility of female staff and more equitable interactions between female and male staff was significant in creating new possibilities for gender roles and relations in BRAC communities. Similarly, there is a visible thread in efforts to apply principles and processes of staff GQAL in community GQAL from 1999 onwards, with positive gender-equality outcomes for women and men, and, in the case of GQAL–CFPR–TUP, gender-equality results contributing to overall programme performance.

While some programmes and gender-equality outcomes lend themselves to quantitative analysis, gender practitioners and evaluators have highlighted that the dominant metrics and methodologies for gathering 'evidence' and determining 'value for money' are not necessarily the most appropriate for assessing all gender-equality outcomes, especially more intangible dimensions such as women's and girls' empowerment, social-norm change or violence against women and girls. Frustrations have been voiced about the reliance on experimental methods, which effectively excludes a large body of both quantitative and qualitative information from the dialogue on 'what works'. Questions are asked about 'Who defines what matters?', 'Who defines and determines "value"?', and how measurement approaches might ensure that women's and men's voices are part of the process that defines 'value'.

A recent article examining the two-decade history of the Safe Motherhood Initiative (SMI) provides an illuminating picture of gender advocates negotiating the vicissitudes of the evidence and 'value for money' agendas (Storeng and Béhague, 2014). To bolster SMI's authority in the global health arena, policy advocates pushed for the need to produce convincing (experimental) evidence and demonstrate value for money. This required a considerable shift in priorities and tactics for the group. Whereas SMI began with an emphasis on poor women's health based on rights and social justice arguments, and on promoting broad-scale action, tactics shifted to simple, targeted interventions for quicker results and more easily measurable interventions. These included dispensing drug-based treatments for common maternal health problems rather than strengthening health systems or training midwives. This strategy shift meant that less attention was paid to the political and structural changes that were needed to address the systemic health inequities that contribute to maternal mortality. Similar concerns have been voiced about narrowly framed women's economic empowerment programmes, where outcomes are measured primarily in relation to increased income rather than in the context of a broader range of outcomes that are less easily measured (e.g., transformation in power, agency and social norms, and women's economic advancement and empowerment) (Taylor and Pereznieto, 2014: 248).

If we recall the analysis presented in relation to the Gender at Work Analytical Framework, gender-equality change requires working across all four quadrants. Addressing discriminatory social norms is key to addressing women's subordination, and implementing programmes that target the upper-right quadrant of the Framework, together with those that target the lower-left quadrant, shows promise in addressing the whole picture of women's empowerment. If we focus exclusively, for example, on the top-right quadrant (resources) simply because these types of interventions are more easily measured, the danger is that programmes and approaches that have the potential to catalyse transformative social change may not be funded. While

> development organizations of all kinds should be looking for the best value for money for marginalized people, [they also] need to understand the scope of the changes that are needed and ensure spending is targeted in ways which genuinely support women living in poverty to challenge inequality in social and political arenas as well as in the marketplace.
>
> (Bowman and Sweetman, 2014: 204)

Across the sector, demands for quantitative data are increasing, given that numbers can be framed as 'value for money' in ways that analyses and anecdotal evidence gleaned from qualitative data cannot (Eyben *et al.*, 2013). In light of this, there has been increased demand for recognition of the value that can be adduced from qualitative data and for the need for a balance of mixed methods in evaluation, 'to better understand the complexity of international development interventions and ... [in] recognition of the fact that no single evaluation methodology can fully capture and measure the multiple processes and outcomes that every development programme involves' (Bamberger, 2013: 1).

Indeed, there is growing consensus around the need for mixed-methods approaches to evaluating the impact of programmes, including gender-equality programmes, that seek transformational change. As we saw in Chapter 4, many of the community GQAL evaluations used multiple methods to understand programme outcomes and impact. A recent review of methods to evaluate women's economic empowerment programmes endorsed mixed-methods evaluations in its conclusion, arguing that they 'lead to more useful findings, as they consider not only the effects of interventions, but also the underlying reasons why they occur'. The authors go on to say that this analysis 'is especially important for Women and Girls' Economic Empowerment (WGEE) projects, as changes in norms, attitudes and behaviours are difficult to fully understand with quantitative data alone' (Taylor and Pereznieto, 2014: 1).

In addition to calling for mixed-methods approaches, those working to strengthen monitoring and evaluation of gender-equality programmes are drawing attention to the need to bring in complexity thinking and to prioritize learning as a key aspect of making sense of programme processes and outcomes – in other words, of deepening our understanding of how gender-equality change happens (Batliwala and Pittman, 2010; Wallace *et al.*, 2013; Miller and Haylock, 2014).

Approaches to monitoring and evaluating gender equality need to take into account, for example, that this type of social change is complex and messy, rather than try to generalize or oversimplify it. In some ways, this thinking has permeated programme evaluation in the community GQAL Programme, though the emphasis is largely on summoning evidence of impact against clearly defined results.

Progress towards gender equality and transforming gender power relations does not always follow a linear or predictable trajectory. Indeed, it confounds the logic of many results-based management and attribution-seeking causal frameworks. This means that measurements and analyses of gender-equality change must be able to capture and interpret backlashes and resistance to change as possible evidence of impact and effectiveness, not necessarily of failure. Additionally, in some instances, merely maintaining the status quo may be evidence of success (Batliwala and Pittman, 2010: 6; Batliwala, 2011: 5). While there may be some 'quick wins' in terms of access to resources, attitudinal and behavioural change and some less 'sticky' norms, overall gender-equality change, particularly in relation to programmes targeting deeply entrenched social norms, may be visible only over the long term:

> Observable changes in people's attitudes and behaviour towards gender norms and in concrete improvements in outcomes for women and girls may well take a generation or more to achieve. Even putting aside the difficulties of attributing the contribution of individual programmes to social change, this means that a programme's higher level 'success' and the robustness of assumed causal connections cannot be tested within the conventional period of one to four years.
>
> (O'Neil, 2016: 28)

Drawing on Denney and Domingo (2015), O'Neil (2016: 28) goes on to argue that theories of change about what contributes to women's empowerment or to reductions in gender inequality need to be broken down into smaller chunks, 'so that programmes identify realistic timeframes and indicators for changes at different stages'. Interim changes in work to address gender norms, for example, might be defined as gaining the support of religious leaders, or as changes in legal/policy reform, with some indication of changes in the attitudes and/or behaviour of men and community leaders (towards greater domestic responsibility, support for women's leadership, etc.). These can be seen as pathways to more profound changes in norms and gender relations.

These conclusions are particularly relevant to the community GQAL Programme. As we saw in Chapter 4, evaluations of the programme showed changes in attitudes and, to some extent, in behaviours (i.e., 'interim' changes), but were not always able to establish whether behavioural changes were sustained and to what extent programme interventions were contributing to social-norm change in participating communities. In view of the argument above, this difficulty is not surprising. It suggests that, for long-term social-change projects, there need to be signposts or markers of short-, medium- and long-term change within the framework of overall assessments of programme 'success'.

From the observations above about what is different in measuring gender-equality change (or other social-transformation efforts), the conclusion is that flexible, adaptive and participative monitoring and evaluation approaches are needed. O'Neil (2016: 25), in making the linkage between gender equality and adaptive development, elaborates: 'causal complexity means that the potential response to a problem may be unclear at the outset', so 'programmes need to be open to experimentation in order to seek to learn from different possible solutions and/or strategies for achieving them'. The building blocks for systematic learning and adaptation include a problem-driven approach and structure learning processes with regular feedback loops.

Returning to the story of GQAL, we can see its value in relation to current concerns about embracing complexity and the importance of building and applying problem-solving skills in implementation, monitoring, evaluation and learning processes. Many of the practices that are identified as promising related to modelling programme learning and adaptation have been tried and tested in GQAL (both among staff and within BRAC communities). The story of GQAL in the community provides a compelling narrative of how processes of learning and adaptation gave rise to an increasingly sophisticated programme that responded to new analyses of what it would take to shift gender equality at multiple levels and among a wider group of stakeholders than originally envisaged.

There were and remain ongoing considerations about how gender-equality outcomes are measured in GQAL. One of the reasons for carrying out the GQAL staff study in 2015 was to build a stronger evidential base about the impact of the programme on participants and the organization. There had been various earlier efforts at evaluation, and, as Chapters 2 and 3 have demonstrated, efforts to document the process and its outcomes. Nevertheless, in looking back at our experience with GQAL with staff and with new understanding of what is possible, we recognize that the process would have benefited from better monitoring and evaluation. When GQAL was implemented, the robust measurement of baseline and end-of-programme attitudes, skills and behaviours that typically characterizes BRAC programme piloting was not prominent in its design. This was partly because GQAL was not focused on VOs or other programme beneficiaries – the most important focus of BRAC. Staff values surveys or more comprehensive knowledge, attitude and practice (KAP) surveys could have been used from the outset, complemented, for example, by systematic monitoring and evaluation through regular case studies and focus group discussions.

Being clearer about expected results, in terms of changes in staff and management attitudes and behaviour, and in terms of higher-level policy and work practices, would have facilitated data collection and helped us to fine-tune the action-learning and organizational systems-change process on the basis of that data (although, as we saw in Chapters 2 and 3, the GQAL staff process did include regular feedback loops that enabled adjustments to the process). It also would have demystified the process for staff, allowing managers, in particular, to understand better how and why the change process worked, so it could be applied to other programmatic areas and organizational issues. If a similar programme were to be implemented today, it would be important to plan and research its impact as thoroughly as BRAC does for its other programmes, to be able to speak sooner and more comprehensively about its impact, and to build a local body of knowledge about promoting gender equality in organizations.

Of course, there is a tension here between the need for clear outcomes and the emergent, non-prescriptive nature of the programme, which, as we have argued, is one of its strengths. Nevertheless, tracking impact in a manner that is true to the spirit of the learning process would be important.

What are the messages for theory and practice in other organizations?

We believe that the GQAL story makes a contribution to both the theory and the practice of changing organizations and communities to advance a gender-equality agenda. We believe there are four main messages:

- There has been considerable recent attention on the importance of norms (World Bank, 2011). Institutional blocks to gender equality are real, but the GQAL staff process is one example of how to change institutional norms in local settings (Area Offices and communities). GQAL was able to change personal beliefs and challenge local norms by facilitating face-to-face discussions among women and men, who talked about issues that mattered to them.
- GQAL strongly supports adaptive development's principle of focusing on problems, not on existing (often imported) solutions. Staff GQAL groups

defined each problem in their terms and took action that made sense in their cultural context. Similarly, in community GQAL, although there was more 'teaching' of gender-equality ideas, participants decided on what actions to take. Both are examples of experience trumping theory and both recognize the importance of context.

- We believe that the GQAL story supports the idea that internal cultural change and learning are required for strategic change related to constituencies. Even though staff GQAL did not continue after 2002, and was limited to Area Offices and not extended to management levels, it had a noticeable impact on individual attitudes and the cultures of Area Offices. It extended its influence in two directions. First, the methodology of GQAL was extended to VOs, the CFPR–TUP and then to a stand-alone programme. Second, GQAL made gender equality a 'thing' at BRAC. It led to a variety of gender-sensitive policies, including the gender policy, the expansion of GQAL to the community, a gender goal in the strategic plan, gender focal points, a gender-responsive policy procedure, a gender lens in auditing programmes, a sexual harassment policy and process, the Gender Equality and Diversity Team, a day-long retreat for the Governing Board to discuss gender issues, and many other changes (see Appendix 6 for a complete list). Participants and leaders from the GQAL Programme implemented many of these policy and programmatic changes. For example, when Sheepa Hafiza was Director of Human Resources and GJD, she was able to implement and interpret a number of gender-related policies and programmes.

- We also believe that the GQAL story illustrates the importance of the smart organizational politics described by O'Neil (2016). The programme began with the sponsorship of the Executive Director and enjoyed his support throughout, but contrary to much advice on organizational change, this was not enough in itself. The programme was as much negotiated as designed; compromises were made; and considerable energy was devoted to responding to issues raised by managers. Our 'political knitting' ensured we remained in touch with and responded to important political currents within BRAC. This has been true from the beginning to the present day.

Given the importance of 'strategic mainstreaming' and its role in the post-2015 agenda, some reflection on the BRAC experience is worthwhile. Although BRAC gender staff brought gender equality to a variety of programmes and organizational forums over the course of two decades, it was only in 2015 that BRAC formally embarked on a gender-mainstreaming journey. The evolution of BRAC's gender-equality programme illustrates some of the tensions and trade-offs that are common to large development organizations that aim to promote gender equality. The first is the tension between stand-alone programming for gender equality and women's empowerment – that is, programmes whose primary or sole purpose is to contribute to gender equality and women's empowerment (GEWE), such as the third stand-alone phase of GQAL, described in this book – and efforts to ensure that all programmes contribute to GEWE, or at least do not worsen women's position or condition. Stand-alone programmes constitute a minuscule percentage of all aid flows, usually less than 5 per cent, and direct support for equality-seeking organizations represent even less – just 0.3 per cent of OECD spending on aid.[8] Therefore, equality advocates have pushed hard for attention to women and gender equality in all development co-operation. This was the thrust of the Beijing Declaration in 1995 and it has remained a focus for advocacy efforts ever since.

But bringing gender-equality dimensions into other types of programmes – for example, education – generates a host of other problems. The most common issue is that such programming requires two different types of expertise: gender-equality expertise and subject-matter expertise. For example, in BRAC, the Gender Justice Team suggested that the curriculum material in BRAC primary schools should present non-stereotypical gender roles and promote gender equality. Doing this well requires detailed knowledge of the whole curriculum for the entirety of a child's schooling and ensuring that any changes are suited to the intellectual development of the child – not too advanced, not too simple, engaging and presented in a way that ordinary teachers will feel comfortable delivering. No gender generalist is likely to know all this, but she/he can critique the existing curriculum. The curriculum developers are also unlikely to have the time to develop this type of specialized expertise without any need for additional resources. This gap is very hard to bridge without fostering long-term collaboration. There is no pay-off for long-term collaboration when accountability is maintained through departmental silos and efficiency pressures are great.

This gap is one of the reasons why the GQAL–CFPR–TUP collaboration was so innovative. The gender-learning dimensions were carefully researched and built on the experience with BRAC staff, and the GQAL facilitators learned enough about the gender dimensions of CFPR–TUP to offer helpful observations about any adjustments that might promote gender equality. The additional cost to the CFPR–TUP Programme of collaborating with GQAL was marginal: BRAC's Chief Financial Officer calculated it at less than 4 per cent of the total CFPR–TUP budget. This additional cost can be justified merely on the basis that CFPR–TUP results were better when there was collaboration with GQAL, let alone on the pro-equality changes in social norms and behaviour at the individual and community levels.

This type of collaboration is rare,[9] not only because it requires certain interpersonal skills among the staff, but also because different professional backgrounds form different mindsets that make mutual understanding challenging. Corporate management and work-practice systems often favour non-integrated ways of working, on the assumption that these will be more efficient and cost-effective. The thinking is that work in silos is easier to control and manage. It may be that GQAL-like discussions and structures would be able to bridge those differences in mindsets and allow staff to design solutions across organizational silos.

Limitations

We are not sure about the word 'limitations'. It implies that something should have been done, but was not. We believe it is more reasonable to focus on what was achieved and to understand that in the context of what was possible at the time. Remembering that BRAC existed in a patriarchal society and that in the early days of the programme those views were held by many BRAC staff allows us to see the programme as very much the art of the possible.

Nevertheless, as many respondents in the 2015 review mentioned limitations, we repeat them here:

- GQAL would have had more of an impact if it had been experienced in some form by regional and senior managers. This would have given such managers more understanding of what was happening below them and built their skills for changing the broader culture of BRAC.
- Staff GQAL could have been renewed and redesigned in order to continue to change both personal attitudes and Area Office work cultures. Given staff turnover and the early cessation of the programme, only a very small percentage of current BRAC staff have been through GQAL.
- Better measurement and understanding of milestones towards normative transformation could have strengthened programme learning and supported and contributed to a better understanding, on the part of managers, of the kinds of outcomes that could be expected, given the timeframe of the interventions.
- BRAC could have developed GQAL into more of a mainstreaming programme that brought this type of analysis to programmes across the organization. That said, gender advocates did bring gender considerations to a wide variety of BRAC initiatives over the years (see Appendix 6), and BRAC has recently implemented a gender-mainstreaming approach in several sectoral programmes (including Education, Health, Micro-finance and Community Empowerment).

Final words

GQAL has been a serious and sustained effort, over two decades, to change the attitudes of BRAC staff, the cultures of Area Offices and the gendered power relations in Bangladeshi communities. Some 16,000 BRAC staff in 800 Area Offices were part of the staff GQAL Programme. Later, the community GQAL Programme reached 390,000 households. This book has documented important changes in both BRAC's staff and beneficiary communities. The review that underlies this book and the various studies conducted over the years have led us to the following conclusions:

- Staff GQAL had a strong and lasting impact on the participants (both women and men). Respondents clearly remembered both the sessions and what they learned 11 years later.

- Staff GQAL changed norms and behaviour in many of the Area Offices with regard to power relations between women and men. For example, there was less harassment and more collegial decision-making between women and men.
- GQAL led to a host of gender-related policy and programme innovations, notably in the area of sexual harassment.
- Although staff GQAL led to normative and behavioural changes at the Area Office level, it is unclear to what extent those normative changes have been sustained since the programme was suspended in 2002.
- Community GQAL led to changes in local norms and behaviour regarding women's decision-making, food sharing and, notably, domestic violence.

We believe that key factors contributing to the success of GQAL through the years were: the leadership of F.H. Abed; the determination of the gender staff; and a methodology, developed by the BRAC Gender Team, that allowed staff and community members to highlight problems in a supportive space and take collective action to change oppressive gender norms.

Notes

1 'Change is Possible' (2013) is the title of an unpublished paper by Sheepa Hafiza.
2 For a complete discussion of GQAL outcomes, see Chapters 3 and 4, this volume.
3 This framework was first developed in Rao and Kelleher (1997).
4 During the early days of GQAL, a BRAC senior manager insisted that development could not be accomplished by men alone. He equated the exclusion of women to running a race with only one leg.
5 For example, if the training were related to teamwork, then evaluation and rewards would have to value team-related behaviours, not just individual ones.
6 Personal communication, December 2016.
7 For a description of the 'Hawthorne studies', see www.boundless.com/management/textbooks/boundless-management-textbook/organizational-theory-3/behavioral-perspectives-30/the-human-side-hawthorne-170-8381/.
8 For more details, see a recent report by the Organization for Economic Co-operation and Development (OECD) on women's rights organizations at www.oecd.org/dac/gender-development/OECD-report-on-womens-rights-organisations.pdf.
9 The Swiss Agency for Development Cooperation tried this and achieved considerable success in its agricultural programme in Cuba.

References

Alvesson, M., Billing, Y.D. (2009) *Understanding Gender and Organizations*, London: Sage.

Bamberger, M. (2013) *The Mixed Methods Approach to Evaluation*, SI Concept Note Series, Arlington, VA: Social Impact.

Batliwala, S. (2011) *Strengthening Monitoring and Evaluation for Women's Rights: Thirteen Insights for Women's Organizations*, Toronto: AWID.

Batliwala, S., Pittman, A. (2010) *Capturing Change in Women's Realities: A Critical Overview of Current Monitoring and Evaluation Frameworks and Approaches*, Toronto: AWID.

Beckhard, R. (1969) *Organisation Development: Strategies and Models*, Reading: Addison-Wesley.

Beer, M., Findstrom, M., Shrader, D. (2016) 'Why Leadership Training Fails and What to Do about It', *Harvard Business Review*, October: 50–57.

Bowman, K., Sweetman, C. (2014) 'Introduction to Gender, Monitoring, Evaluation and Learning', *Gender and Development*, 22.2: 201–212.

Brouwers, R. (2013) 'Revisiting Gender Mainstreaming in International Development: Goodbye to an Illusionary Strategy', Working Paper No. 556, The Hague: Institute of Social Studies.

Cameron, K.S., Quinn, R.E. (2006) *Diagnosing and Changing Organisational Culture*, revised edition, San Francisco: Jossey-Bass.

Cohen, S., Sachdeva, N., Taylor, S., Cortes, P. (2013) *Gender Mainstreaming Approaches in Development Programming: Being Strategic and Achieving Results in an Evolving Development Context*, New York: UN Women.

Denney, L., Domingo, P. (2015) *Future Directions of Security and Justice: Context-relevant, Flexible and Transnational Programming?*, London: ODI.

Derbyshire, H., Dolata, N., Ahluwalia, K. (2015) *Untangling Gender Mainstreaming: A Theory of Change Based on Experience and Reflection*, London: Gender and Development Network, http://gadnetwork.org/gadn-resources/2015/3/6/untangling-gender-mainstreaming-a-theory-of-change-based-on-experience-and-reflection (accessed 28 February 2017).

DFID (n.d.) 'Guidance on Monitoring and Evaluation for Programming on Violence against Women and Girls', Guidance Note 3, Chase Guidance Note Series, London: DFID. www.gov.uk/government/uploads/system/uploads/attachment_data/file/67334/How-to-note-VAWG-3-monitoring-eval.pdf (accessed 10 December 2016).

Eyben, R., Guijit, I., Roche, C., Shutt, C., Whitty, B. (2013) *The Politics of Evidence*, conference report for 'The Big Push Forward', Institute of Development Studies, Sussex, 23–24 April. http://bigpushforward.net/wp-content/uploads/2013/09/BPF-PoE-conference-report.pdf (accessed 10 December 2016).

Fleming, F. (2013) 'Evaluation Methods for Assessing Value for Money', Australasian Evaluation Society. http://betterevaluation.org/sites/default/files/Evaluating%20methods%20for%20assessing%20VfM%20-%20Farida%20Fleming.pdf (accessed 8 December 2016).

Ignatief, M., Guttman, A. (2003) *Human Rights as Politics and Idolatry*, Princeton: Princeton University Press.

Jackson, P. (2012) *Value for Money and International Development: Deconstructing Myths to Promote a More Constructive Discussion*, OECD Development Assistance Committee. www.oecd.org/dac/ (accessed 13 December 2016).

Jahan, F., Shahan, A., Khan, S., Akter-uz-zaman, S., Jahan, M. (2016) 'Gender Quality Action and Learning Programme: Documenting the Transformations Achieved and the Process of Achieving Them', unpublished evaluation report, Dhaka: BRAC.

Jewkes, R., Flood, M., Lang, J. (2014) 'From Work with Men and Boys to Changes of Social Norms and Reductions of Inequities in Gender Relations: A Conceptual Shift in Prevention of Violence against Women and Girls', *Lancet*, 385.9977: 1580–1589.

Kegan, R., Lahey, L.L. (2009) *Immunity to Change: How to Overcome it and Unlock Potential in Yourself and Your Organization*, Cambridge, MA: Harvard Business Press.

Kelleher, D., Finestone, P., Lowy, A. (1986) 'Managerial Learning: First Notes from an Unstudied Frontier', *Group and Organization Management*, 11.3: 169–202.

Mackay, F. (2011) 'Conclusion: Towards a Feminist Institutionalism?' in M.L. Krook and F. Mackay (eds), *Gender, Politics and Institutions: Towards a Feminist Institutionalism*, Basingstoke: Palgrave Macmillan.

Mackay, F., Kenny, M., Chappell, L. (2010) 'New Institutionalism through a Gender Lens: Towards a Feminist Institutionalism?', *International Political Science Review*, 31.5: 573–588. Mahmud, S., Sultan, M., Huq, L. (2012) *Assessing the Performance of GQAL in Changing Gender Norms and Behaviour*, BDI Research Report No. 1, Dhaka: BRAC Development Institute.

Miller, C., Haylock, L. (2014) 'Capturing Changes in Women's Lives: The Experiences of Oxfam Canada in Applying Feminist Evaluation Principles to Monitoring and Evaluation Practices', *Gender and Development*, 22.2: 291–310.

Milward, K., Mukhopadhyay, M., Wong, F. (2015) 'Gender Mainstreaming Critiques: Signposts or Dead Ends?', *IDS Bulletin*, 46.4: 75–81.

Molyneux, M. (2010) 'Mobilization without Emancipation: Women's Interests, the State, and Revolution in Nicaragua' in M.L. Krook and S. Childs (eds), *Women, Gender and Politics: A Reader*, Oxford: Oxford University Press.

Mukhopadhyay, M., Wong, F. (2007) *Revisiting Gender Training: The Making and Remaking of Gender Knowledge: A Global Sourcebook*, Amsterdam: KIT.

Nazneen, S. (2007) 'Gender Sensitive Accountability of Service Delivery NGOs: BRAC and PROSHIKA in Bangladesh', D.Phil. dissertation, Brighton: University of Sussex.

ODI (2014) *Gender Justice and Social Norms: Processes of Change for Adolescent Girls*, London: ODI.

O'Neil, T. (2016) *Using Adaptive Development to Support Feminist Action*, London: ODI.

Rao, A., Cloud, H., Staudt, K. (1991) *Gender Training and Development Planning: Learning from Experience*, conference report, Bergen.

Rao, A., Kelleher, D. (eds) (1997) *Power: A Trialogue*, Washington, DC: AWID.

Rao, A., Sandler, J., Kelleher, D., Miller, C. (2016) *Gender at Work: Theory and Practice for 21st Century Organizations*, Abingdon: Routledge.

Reemer, T. (2015) *Examining Pathways towards Engendered Change Involving Men and Women in Care Work in West Nile, Uganda*, Oxford: Oxfam.

Scharmer, C.O. (2009) *Theory U: Learning from the Future as it Emerges*, San Francisco: Berrett-Koehler.

Schein, E.H. (2004) *Organizational Culture and Leadership*, 3rd edition, New York: John Wiley & Sons.

Smith, L.C., Kahn, F., Frankenberger, T.R., Wadud, A. (2011) 'Admissible Evidence in the Court of International Development Evaluation? The Impact of CARE's SHOUHARDO Project on Child Stunting in Bangladesh', IDS Working Paper No. 376, Brighton: IDS.

Storeng, K.T., Béhague, B.T. (2014) '"Playing the Numbers Game": Evidence Based Advocacy and the Technical Narrowing of the Safe Motherhood Initiative', *Medical Anthropology Quarterly*, 28.2: 260–279.

Taylor, M. (2011) *Emergent Learning for Wisdom*, New York: Palgrave.

Taylor, G., Pereznieto, P. (2014) *Review of Evaluation Approaches and Methods Used by Interventions on Women and Girls' Economic Empowerment*, London: ODI.

UN Women (2015) *Review of Corporate Gender Equality Evaluations in the United Nations System*, New York: UN Women. www.unwomen.org/en/digital-library/publications/2015/7/review-of-corporate-gender-equality-evaluations-in-the-united-nations-system (accessed 11 December 2016).

UN Women Training Centre (2015) *Training for Gender Equality: 20 Years on*, New York: UN Women.

VeneKlasen, L., Miller, V. (2002) *A New Weave of Power, People and Politics: The Advocacy Guide for Citizen Participation*, Oklahoma City: World Neighbours.

Wallace, T., Porter, F., Ralph-Bowman, M. (2013) *Aid, NGOs and the Realities of Women's Lives: A Perfect Storm*, Bourton on Dunsmore: Practical Action.

Watkins, F. (2004) *DFID's Experience of Gender Mainstreaming: 1995 to 2004*, London: UK Department for International Development.

Weisbord, M. (2012) *Productive Workplaces: Dignity, Meaning and Community in the 21st Century*, San Francisco: Jossey-Bass.

World Bank (2011) *World Development Report: Gender Equality and Development*, Washington, DC: World Bank Group.

World Bank (2014) *Voice and Agency: Empowering Women and Girls for Shared Prosperity*, Washington, DC: World Bank Group.

Appendix 1: BRAC gender-equality milestones

1972   BRAC founded

1973   Sulla Project and formation of women's groups

1975   Women's income generating project (with handicraft producers) in Jamalpur

1991   Women's Advisory Committee (WAC) set up

1993   Gender Awareness and Analysis Course (GAAC) introduced

1994   **Gender Quality Action Learning (GQAL) Team established**; GQAL needs assessment undertaken

1995   UN Fourth World Conference on Women, Beijing; **GQAL Programme for BRAC staff launched**; Women-only recruitment policy announced for the year

1996   GQAL (staff) expanded to 20 Area Offices; Maternity leave (paid and unpaid) introduced

1997   First workshop on sexual harassment; BRAC Values developed with training sessions for staff; Gender policy introduced (revised 2005); Daycare for children of staff introduced

1999   Highest ever (to date) proportion of female staff in BRAC (30 per cent)

2001   GQAL pilot with Village Organization (VO) members under Training Division

2001   **GQAL with VOs relaunched jointly with Research and Evaluation Division**

2003   Gender Unit moved to BRAC Advocacy and Human Rights Unit (BAHRU); Gender training with Executive Director and senior managers

2004   Sexual Harassment Elimination (SHE) policy introduced; Paternity leave policy introduced; *Mon Khule Kotha Bola* forum (listening to female and male staff voices); SHARE (Sexual Harassment Redressal) Unit established; Gender policy and SHE policy staff orientation

2005   **GQAL launched as component of BRAC's Challenging the Frontiers of Poverty Reduction Targeting the Ultra Poor (CFPR–TUP)**; Gender Justice and Diversity (GJD) Unit developed under Human Resources Division; GQAL moved from Training Division to Human Resources; **End of GQAL Programme with staff**

2007   Gender focal points set up to support gender policy implementation; Gender-responsive human resources policy and procedure developed

2009   Gender Justice and Diversity Division established

2010   MEJNIN (Safe Citizenship for Girls) launched (expanded in 2012); GQAL launched as POSITION (Enhancing a Positive Life)

2011   Gender audit; Gender retreat for BRAC's Governing Board; Gender Equality Goal and Action Plan for BRAC approved by BRAC's Governing Board

2012   POSITION renamed GQAL and launched as a stand-alone community programme by GJD; Expansion of GQAL Programme to eight regions

Note: This is not a comprehensive list of gender-equality milestones in BRAC; rather, the focus is on activities referenced in the book.

Appendix 2: Interview schedules and questionnaires

Questions for GQAL Programme participants (managers)

1 What did you do in your GQAL experience?
2 What did you/your group achieve?
3 What was the reason behind the success of GQAL?
4 What problems did you face in implementing GQAL changes?
5 Do you see similar programmes to GQAL now? Which ones? How are they similar? How different?
6 Is there a need for doing a similar programme to GQAL for staff in BRAC? Why? Why not?

Questions for GQAL Programme participants (staff)

1 What did you do in your GQAL experience?
2 What did you/your group achieve?
3 Did your own perceptions or behaviour change as a result of your GQAL experience? If 'yes', can you describe how? Did this change last? Why? Why not?
4 What problems did you face in implementing GQAL changes?
5 Do you see similar programmes to GQAL now? Which ones? How are they similar? How different?
6 Is there a need for doing a similar programme to GQAL for staff in BRAC? Why? Why not?

Questions for GQAL Team and facilitators

1 What was your most memorable experience with GQAL?
2 Do you think it was successful? If 'yes', why? If 'no', why not?
3 What was the biggest hurdle you faced in implementing GQAL?
4 What were the weaknesses of GQAL?
5 In your opinion, what did GQAL achieve?

    a At the organizational culture level

        i Systems, processes and ways of working in BRAC
        ii BRAC programmes
        iii BRAC organizational culture, hierarchy and relationships among staff

b   At the community level

    i   Women's voice within household decision-making
   ii   Attitudes and behaviours of women and men
  iii   Sharing of housework
   iv   Violence against women
    v   Women's mobility and safety
   vi   Asset ownership
  vii   Nutrition
 viii   Leisure time

Appendix 3: List of people interviewed

Current and former senior managers

Sir Fazle Hasan Abed, KCMG, current Chairperson of BRAC and Executive Director in 1994

Dr Mushtaque Chowdury, Vice-Chair and interim Executive Director at the time of the interview, and Director of the Research and Evaluation Division in 1994

Ms Tamara Hasan Abed, Senior Director of BRAC Enterprises

Mr Shameran Abed, Director Micro-finance

Dr Mahbub Hussain, recently retired Executive Director

Dr Samdani Fakir, retired, Director of Training in 1994

Dr Salehuddin Ahmed, retired, Deputy Director of BRAC in 1994

Mr Sadequr Rahman Khan, Head of Training, member of GQAL lead team in 1994

Mr Riaz Uddin, Head of Micro-finance, regional manager in 1994

Managers who participated in GQAL

R.M. Forhad

Humayun Kabir

Harashit Mondal

Anwara Khatun

Md. Shafiqul Islam

Rokeya Khatun

Hafiza Khatun

Branch and Area Office staff who participated in GQAL

Shova Sarkar

Razia Begum

Md. Nurul Islam

Nadira Begum

Dipti Majumder

Md. Abdus Sabur
Rawshanara Begum
M. Humayun Kabir
Runu Rani Saha
Sahida Akhter
Shirin Afrose
Sulekha Akhter
Khodeza Begum
Gokul Chandra Sarker

GQAL trainers

Ratna Guha
Sayra Banu
Fazlul Huq
Anirudhdha Guha
Samina Sultana
Nazma Akhter Khanom
Md. Shah Alam
Sultan Mahmood
Afroza Khan
Md. Habibur Rahman
Rokeya Begum

Appendix 4: Staff GQAL survey questionnaire (English version)

1 From 1995–2000 which BRAC programme did you work with (please mention the name sequentially)?

    1   ......
    2   ......
    3   ......

2 From 1995–2000, which areas did you work in (please mention the name sequentially)?

    1   ......
    2   ......
    3   ......

3 When did you join in BRAC?

    Year ......

4 What was your level in BRAC during 2000?

    ......

5 Did you participate in BRAC staff GQAL training?

    1   Yes
    2   No (The interview session must end if the answer is 'No'.)

6 Where did you receive staff GQAL?

    1   Branch Office/Area Office ......
    2   Outpost ......

7 Which problems did your Branch/Area Office take initiatives to solve?

    1   Relationships between men and women
    2   Office-related rule and regulation/decision
    3   BRAC beneficiaries
    4   Cannot recall
    5   Others

8   Did your Branch/Area Office's initiatives solve the problem?

    1   Did not work
    2   Worked for some time
    3   The solution became the usual way of working
    4   Cannot remember

9   To solve identified problems, our managers

    1   Listened, but did not accept our ideas
    2   Gave us liberty to implement but were not supportive
    3   Tried our ideas, but were not supportive
    4   Practised new learning and supported us
    5   Cannot remember
    6   I did not need to go to manager regarding this matter (when the respondent is manager)

Please rate each of the following aspects of the GQAL training in which you participated

1   Understanding women and men in our society without falling into harmful stereotypes

    1   Not important
    2   Less important
    3   Slightly important
    4   Very important
    5   Cannot remember

2   Learning how to analyse problems

    1   Not important
    2   Less important
    3   Slightly important
    4   Very important
    5   Cannot remember

3   Practising more respectful relationships with peers, managers and BRAC clients

    1   Not important
    2   Less important
    3   Slightly important
    4   Very important
    5   Cannot remember

4   Taking greater responsibility and initiative for problem-solving

    1   Not important
    2   Less important

3   Slightly important
4   Very important
5   Cannot remember

5   Working better as a team with colleagues and managers

1   Not important
2   Less important
3   Slightly important
4   Very important
5   Cannot remember

The GQAL training (give a tick in relevant answer)

1   Changed my ideas about what women and men can do and be

1   Not at all
2   Slightly
3   Somewhat
4   To a great extent

2   Developed my problem-solving skills

1   Not at all
2   Slightly
3   Somewhat
4   To a great extent

3   Permanently changed how I work with others

1   Not at all
2   Slightly
3   Somewhat
4   To a great extent

4   Encouraged me to take initiatives to solve problems

1   Not at all
2   Slightly
3   Somewhat
4   To a great extent

5   Please share any other comments about the impact on you and on BRAC of the GQAL training.

......

6   Please tell us if you think the BRAC GQAL training is still relevant for BRAC today, and explain why you think so.

......

7   If you would like to be interviewed about your experience with BRAC's GQAL Programme, please share your contact information

- Name:
- Email:
- Telephone number:

Appendix 5: Criteria for issue selection

To be eligible for selection, an issue must meet **each one** of the three criteria described below. Meeting only one or two of the criteria will not be sufficient.

1 Gender relevance

We need to examine and compare the issues to determine whether working on them will help BRAC and/or BRAC staff to empower poor women by increasing their:

- access to resources such as credit, free time, technology, knowledge/skills, land, etc.;
- access to and control of benefits such as income;
- status;
- decision-making power;
- control of their bodies/health;
- mobility/safety;
- ability to know and negotiate for their rights;
- reduce conflict between women and men customers;
- retain good female staff;
- improve working relationships between women and men staff;
- reduce conflict between work and family for women and men staff.

If working on an issue does not relate to making improvements in any of these areas, it should not be selected.

2 Importance

An issue is important if:

- it is important for all members of the Gender Action Learning Team;
- it is useful for BRAC to work on this issue;
- it has potential to lead to sustainable and/or replicable change;
- it is a current issue (not out of date).

If the issue is not important based on this definition, it should not be selected.

3 Contribution

This criterion helps the Gender Action Learning Team to decide whether the team can work to improve the issue. Examples of possible improvements include:

- collecting useful and reliable information about the issue or its causes and effects;
- implementation of improvements in attitude, behaviour or skills by the team members based on their GQAL learning;
- improving communication to share learning with other parts and levels of BRAC;
- increased team ownership and responsibility for helping to problem-solve (instead of merely naming problems and shifting responsibility);
- practical recommendations for improvements to other concerned levels of BRAC.

Many issues are complex and require action for improvement by different levels of BRAC. If the team cannot explain how they themselves are part of the problem and/or how they might contribute to an improvement, they should not select the issue.

Appendix 6: Steps towards gender mainstreaming, 1994–2016

1991–present	Capacity-building/action learning is held with all BRAC staff to develop relevant gender understanding and analytical skills.
1994	Beginning of GQAL (Research, Evaluation and Development (RED) process starts in 2002).
1996–present	International Women's Day observations with all HQ and field staff.
2004	Gender analysis of Water, Sanitation and Hygiene (WASH) country-wide programmes is completed to include analyses of practical and strategic interests of women and girls.
2005	Human Resources Division is launched, together with the Gender, Justice and Diversity (GJD) Unit; gender-responsive policy is instituted and the *Mon Khule Kotha Bola* forum is convened.
2006	Gender Analysis Framework is developed for WASH; mainstreaming of menstruation hygiene management at school. A BRAC-wide gender indicator is developed for the RED Department to monitor programmes. International Women's Day celebration is held with BRAC partners. It features a community gathering, motorcycle relay, posters, banners and rally and supports information-sharing, learning and negotiation around issues. Participants include other NGOs, university students and representatives of local and national government.
2006–2007	Gender focal points are designated to help implement the gender policy across BRAC programmes and departments.
2006–2008	Orientation is held for staff of BRAC's Human Rights and Legal Education (HRLE) Programme; includes three days of GQAL.
2007	BRAC audit is launched, using a gender lens. Gender Equality and Diversity Team (GEDT) is formed, consisting of BRAC senior leaders, who are engaged in strategic thinking and decision-making regarding gender equality.

2008   Capacity-building is conducted with all managers of the WASH Programme (one-time training including action-learning approach to track expected change). Field-based gender sensitization training is launched for some field offices to identify and address gender issues and make follow-up commitments. GJD's gender trainers are responsible for tracking progress and following up with individual offices.

2009–2011   Capacity-building is held for all CFPR–TUP staff so that they can promote selected methodologies of GQAL in new areas.

2010   *Mon Khule Kotha Bola* forum is held and gender training is conducted for Aarong and the Ayesha Abed Foundation (AAF) with staff, artisans and production workers. The focus of these initiatives is to create a gender-responsive institutional culture.

2010–2011   BRAC conducts a gender audit, which generates recommendations for developing programmatic goals related to gender.

2011   BRAC's Governing Board members call for a day-long gender retreat to share findings of the gender audit and improve understanding of BRAC's gender work. The Board approves the first-ever BRAC Gender Equality Goal and identifies priorities at the organizational and programmatic level. Twenty-two programmes and departments develop their own Gender Equality Action Plans and report on their progress to the Executive Director and Governing Board. Work begins with BRAC's Education Programme to review curriculum, learning material and modules with a gender lens and develop gender and ethics outcome indicators. Guidelines are developed for reviewing any communications related to the curriculum and an orientation is given to all relevant staff. Classroom gender tracker is developed. Gender sensitivity training is conducted with all schoolteachers, health workers and Human Rights and Legal Aid Sevices (HRLS) *shebikas* (volunteers), WASH committee members, other community members, as well as BRAC project staff working under the new Integrated Development Programme (IDP) in very remote, poor and waterlogged or otherwise geographically inaccessible areas.

2012   F.H. Abed, former Executive Director and Chairperson of BRAC, declares gender the one unfinished agenda of his life.

2013–2015   Community Empowerment Programme (CEP) and other programmes launch using techniques from GQAL, such as community and tea stall meetings. The IDP integrates the GQAL model, providing GQAL training to selected couples and men and women from each Village Development Committee (VDC). Training sessions are held for approximately 46,000 men and women in four sub-districts of *haor* areas (Baniachang, Derai, Itna and Khaliajury). At the end of the training, participants declare their joint commitment to the principles of GQAL. The trained couples and other participants meet every three months and share the learning with their neighbours.

2014   The BRAC Education Programme (BEP) incorporates the MEJNIN Programme and works with 37 schools in two sub-districts of Sylhet. GQAL develops cost-effective interventions for micro-finance.

2016   BRAC adopts 'Gender transformative change to create greater voice, choice, and spaces for women across all BRAC's programmes' as strategic goal. From September, the Community Empowerment Programme integrates a customized model of GQAL. It focuses on involving the Ending Violence Against Women Committee (EVAWC) and appointing Youth Gender Justice Educators in the Polli Somaj areas. The training will be provided to the men, women and youth of EVAWC and the Youth Committee. This action is launched in 12 sub-districts. Also from September, under the banner of the CEP, the MEJNIN Programme is integrated into ten new districts. The goal is to cover about 400 schools and reach about 200,000 students, teachers, community members, law-enforcement officers, media representatives, and local and national government representatives by 2020. The IDP starts working on integrating the GQAL model in its work to sensitize the Development Support Group (DSG), a village-based group comprising local elites, teachers, and Village Development Organization (VDO) members. The aim is to support the VDO to change traditional gender norms within the family and society. One hundred staff are trained on the GQAL model, focusing on reducing VAW by engaging men and boys. About 8,000 women and men from the DSG and about 6,600 adolescent girls and boys from the Adolescent Development Programme (ADP) will receive the training. Thereafter, they will draft action plans and commit to challenging traditional gender norms and reducing violence against women and children.

Ongoing   Gender mainstreaming is carried out to improve the physical setting of the Aarong store and its production centres, and to change mindsets among all staff and artisans with an intense focus on ending violence against women and transforming the organizational culture. Currently, Aarong has

60,000 artisans and 3,000 employees. GJD is working in collaboration and partnership with Aarong, dairy enterprises and BRAC sectoral programmes (including Education, Health, Micro-finance, Community Empowerment and IDP) on gender mainstreaming. BRAC's gender strategy is developed, with clear programmatic and organizational goals. Gender analysis is done for the above sectors and commitments are made. Senior managers accept gender commitments and circulate their agreement across all BRAC programmes and enterprises.

2017   BRAC's Road Safety Programme (RSP) implements a gender-sensitive initiative from January 2017. Its main objective is to sensitize bus drivers, drivers' assistants, bus owners, BRTA authorities, government sub-district representatives, district- and national-level Road Safety Committee members, schoolteachers, students and the wider community about sexual harassment on public transport and in public places, and engage them in efforts to reduce such harassment. The initiative will reach about 120,000 people in Gazipur and Dhaka.

Index

Page numbers in bold denote tables. Page numbers in italics denote figures. Page numbers with "n" refer to notes.